10 SECRETS TO BECOMING A WORRY-FREE

Mom

CINDI McMENAMIN

HARVEST HOUSE PUBLISHERS
EUGENE, OREGON

Cover by Dugan Design Group

Cover photo © Stockbroker / Alamy

10 SECRETS TO BECOMING A WORRY-FREE MOM
Copyright © 2016 by Cindi McMenamin
Published by Harvest House Publishers
Eugene, Oregon 97402
www.harvesthousepublishers.com

Library of Congress Cataloging-in-Publication Data
McMenamin, Cindi
10 secrets to becoming a worry-free mom / Cindi McMenamin.
   pages cm
ISBN 978-0-7369-6394-7 (pbk.)
ISBN 978-0-7369-6395-4 (eBook)
1. Mothers—Religious life. 2. Worry—Relicious aspects—Christianity. I. Title. II. Title: Ten secrets of becoming a worry-free mom.
   BV4529.18.M378 2016
   248.8'431—dc23   2015028996

16 17 18 19 20 21 22 23 24 / BP-KBD / 10 9 8 7 6 5 4 3 2 1

*To the Only One who can calm the seas—as well as our fears—
and care for what we love far better than we can:
the Perfect Parent, the Lord Jesus Christ.*

Acknowledgments

My heartfelt thanks to:

- My daughter, Dana, for your patience as I learned to trust God with all that I didn't know about how to be your mom. You turned out wonderfully by His grace. And you really did make this job an easy one.

- My armor-bearing friends—Connie Boyd, Lisa Pacheco, Amber Paulsen, and Barbara Willett—for your encouraging emails and powerful prayers as I struggled through the writing of this book.

- My wise, insightful, and beautifully Christlike college friend, Joani Bell, for giving me practically a whole chapter when I was stuck and needed stories moms can relate to with teaching they can emulate. I hope to be a mom like you someday, Joan.

- My own mom, Joyce, for teaching me to trust in God and take my concerns to Him in prayer.

- My other mom, Sharon, for loving me, Hugh, and Dana as your own.

Contents

The Choice Is Yours. 7

1. What If I'm Not Doing This Right?. 15
   Secret 1: Partnering with the Perfect Parent

2. Be Careful. 37
   Secret 2: Realizing God Can Control What You Can't

3. Why This?. 63
   Secret 3: Trusting God's Unseen Work in Their Lives

4. Will They Ever Get Through This Phase? 81
   Secret 4: Relying on the Unchanging, Immovable God

5. You're Hanging Out with Who? 97
   Secret 5: Giving Their Social Life to God

6. I Wish That Had Never Happened 117
   Secret 6: Trusting God's Faultless Filter

7. You Did What? 137
   Secret 7: Giving Their Poor Decisions to God

8. You're Breaking My Heart. 155
   Secret 8: Trusting God with Their Spiritual Foundation

9. I Wish I Could Do More. 177
   Secret 9: Surrendering to God Your Tendency to Rescue

10. You Want to Do *What* with Your Life? 195
    Secret 10: Trusting God with Their Future

    Appendix A: Drawing Nearer to the Perfect Parent 215

    Appendix B: Daily Guide to Praying for Your Child 217

    Notes. 221

The Choice Is Yours

....

*I*magine never having to worry about your children again.

That would be the life, wouldn't it? No more sleepless nights, stressful days, or a stomach tied up in knots because of what your children are going through that you can't control, or what might happen to them that you constantly fear.

I'm sure you and I would never worry at all if we could be assured that our children would be happy, healthy, and safe all their days. But life comes with no such assurances. And while I personally can't promise the well-being of your children, I can offer you ten "secrets" through this book that I guarantee will change your life—and the lives of those you love—for the better.

The secrets in this book will help you eliminate worry, experience peace, and enjoy the task of parenting no matter how young or old your children are and no matter how much damage they might have done already. I'm not going to present "Ten Secrets to Make Your Child Behave" or "Ten Ways to Ensure They Never Get Hurt." Nor will I suggest how to convince them to make the choices you'd prefer. Instead, I'm going to offer you a partnership that promises peace and a lifestyle of leaning on the One who can do far more for and with your child than you ever could.

I'm inviting you into a partnership with the Living God that will change the way you think and act. And in this partnership, you will find the means to a worry-free, stress-free life.

I realize that by writing those words I am making a pretty big claim. But you see, I've walked through some of the situations you already fear and I've talked with many moms who have already experienced some of the very things you dread. And we've all gone through these situations in a partnership with the Perfect Parent whom we are convinced has our lives and the lives of our children securely in His hands.

Granted, there are so many variables that exist to cause us to worry about our children—their personalities and behavior, their environment, their friends or lack of them, their impulsiveness, their attitudes, their weaknesses, and their disposition toward the things that could derail them from their goals...and ours. There is a world outside their door that is waiting to gobble them up when it comes to destroying their values, challenging their beliefs, and luring them into materialism, greed, and a selfish way of life. Will they make the right decisions in order to succeed in life? Will they be happy and content? Will they hold on to the values you teach them? How will they raise their own children someday?

And what can we, as moms, do about it anyway?

Megan, a mom of four children under the age of seven, says: "I worry so much about my children getting hurt or even worse, dying. I get scared and think the worst. Maybe it's normal, but I don't like that feeling. I worry about when they get older, what they are doing at school, and if their friends are having any negative influences on them. The worry is constant and my kids are so young."

And Sue, the mom of a 19-year-old son, said she has always worried, almost obsessively, over her son's physical safety.

"I worried countless times when he would be out with friends and I wouldn't be able to reach him. My initial response was often a paralyzing and dreadful feeling of fear. Just when I thought I couldn't take it any longer waiting to hear from him, he would text me. I would never wish upon anyone to experience the intense degree of fear I would feel. It was awful."

But you and I were never meant to live that way.

Scripture says God has not given us the spirit of worry or fear, but of power, love, and a sound mind (2 Timothy 1:7). And a mom can have a tremendously positive influence on her child when she is exercising not worry or fear, but God's power, love, and a sound mind.

I know that's the kind of mom you want to be—one who relies on God's power and love, and who has a sound mind.

Megan said, "My trust in God helps me to calm down, but I feel this trust in Him is stronger in other parts of my life, like my marriage and finances. I need to trust more in what God has planned for my children and their futures."

Megan is not alone in how she feels. Many worried moms believe in God. They just don't know how to connect their faith in God with their concern for their children. This book is written to share how you can take that step—one that will make all the difference in your life and your children's. It will show you, in a practical way, how to trust God on a daily basis with what is most important to you.

Trusting God with your children is not just wishful thinking and hoping God agrees with your prayers. This partnership I want to invite you into is a lifestyle of leaning on the Living God who can accomplish all that we cannot, and who can determine what is best for your child when you and I only think we can.

Why the Worry Must Go

Let's begin by looking at what worry does to us, our health, and our relationships.

1. Worry Stresses Us Out

Worry causes stress—and stress kills. Really, it does. Stress not only impacts a woman's health, appearance, relationships, and overall quality of life, stress prematurely ages us. Worry is also linked to ulcers and other health problems. By choosing not to worry, you are investing in your health, which is a gift to yourself and your family.

According to a May 2014 Barna Research report, American moms are stressed, tired, overcommitted, and not sure how best to navigate work and family. While most moms with kids at home say they are satisfied with their family life (61 percent), for many it's also the greatest source of stress. In addition, moms (20 percent) are nearly twice as likely as women without kids (12 percent) to become stressed to the point of physical illness.[1] And worry plays a big part in that.

2. Worry Pushes Our Children Away

One reason children tend to not tell their parents all that is going on in their lives (or not be completely honest with them) is because they "don't want Mom to worry."

While I was writing my book *When a Mom Inspires Her Daughter*, I asked daughters ages 12-40 about their relationships with their moms. Through their answers, I discovered that many daughters, regardless of their ages, said their moms worried about them too much. They knew their moms cared for them, but it concerned them, and at times annoyed them, that their mothers worried so much. By choosing not to worry, you are investing in your relationship with your children as well.

3. Worry Models Mistrust to Our Children

Worry says to our children and others, "God can't work this out." Therefore, worry is the sin of having no confidence in God. I know that you, like me, aren't consciously thinking those words when you worry. But it's what we're communicating.

You don't want to display that type of mistrust to your children. How you live will, to a great degree, impact how your children live. What you worry about, they will tend to worry about. On the flip side of that, where you put your trust will greatly impact how they will choose to handle situations in life too.

Even if your children don't imitate your faith or degree of trust, they will know where they should place their trust. Your choices—including whether you decide to worry or trust God—will speak louder to them than any lecture. Your choices will influence your children's choices well into their adulthood.

The Root of Worry

We tend to think that how much we worry is an indication of how much we love our children. But it is actually an indication of *how little we know God*. Because the more we get to know God as the all-knowing, all-loving, all-wise Perfect Parent, the more easily we will be able to trust Him with what is most important to us and experience peace—even if, right now, you...

- lose sleep at night worrying about where your child is.
- are fearful when it comes to your child's health or well-being.
- find yourself replaying past situations in your mind and thinking you could have responded to your child in a better way.
- are fearful of what the teenage years will hold for your son or daughter.
- are a single mom (or a mom who *feels* like she's raising her children alone).

The Journey Ahead

In this book you will hear from moms who have experienced what they thought was the worst, but saw the Lord come through in amazing ways. And in every chapter, you will discover scriptural principles and practical guidance for eliminating worry from your life and experiencing God's peace.

You will also get a chance, at the end of each chapter, to apply what you've learned individually, as well as in community with other moms. The section called "Becoming a Worry-Free Mom— in Community" is meant for you to work through with another mom or two who also struggles with worry. Or, you can recommend this book for use in a group setting at your church or in someone's home. One of the fastest and most effective ways to give up a destructive habit like worrying is to come alongside others who can share accountability to one another.

Finally, each chapter ends with my prayer for you, or a prayer you can say yourself to help you grow in wisdom, knowledge, and intimacy with Christ so that you can be a worry-free mom and a wonderfully free woman.

Key to making all this happen is having a willingness to surrender your worries to the Lord. How does that happen?

The ABCs of Surrender

- **A** - *Admit you do not have control over your child's life.*
  Yes, you can control his or her form of entertainment,
  friends, and environment for a while. But as good of a
  monitor as you may be, your child will eventually make
  decisions on his or her own. And those decisions may, at
  times, grieve your heart. So give up that quest for control right now by saying aloud, "I am not in control of
  my child's life. God is."

- **B** - *Believe God wants only the best for you* and *your child.* Sometimes we fear that God will ask something of us or our children that we're not willing to give. When you understand that God loves your child even more than you do, and that He loves you more than you can imagine, there is peace in placing yourself and your child in God's hands. After you've admitted you don't have control, take the next step and believe that His control of your life, as well as your child's, is truly a good thing.

- **C -** *Commit yourself to a deeper knowledge of God.* I strongly believe that the extent of our worry is directly related to how well we know God. Notice I didn't say our worrying is related to how well we *trust* God. The reason is this: When we truly know Him and understand all that He is capable of, we can't help but trust Him. Through familiarity and intimate knowledge comes trust. So commit yourself right now to reading through this entire book, completing the application sections, and getting to know God better than you ever have before. As you do, your worries will fall by the wayside. And you'll have a new, healthier habit: trust.

The Choice Is Yours

Are you ready to depend on God to do the heavy lifting with the worries that are weighing you down? You can choose to be controlled by your circumstances (and keep worrying), or you can yield yourself to the One who controls all circumstances.

Choose to be controlled by the still, small voice of the One who can still any storm…the One who beckons you to be still and know that He is God over everything, including your children.

Choose to partner with the Perfect Parent.

1

What If I'm Not Doing This Right?

Secret 1: Partnering with the Perfect Parent

*I*f you've ever thought *What if I'm not doing this right?*, you are not alone.

Every one of us has wondered, at one time or another, if we're up for this task of mothering or if we're just messing up our kids.

What if I'm not involved enough in their lives?

What if I'm holding them back?

What if I'm too strict?

What if I'm not strict enough?

What if my own dysfunction is rubbing off on them?

No, you're not the only mom who wrestles with insecurities and thoughts that you're in over your head. And you're not the only mom who beats yourself up when your children behave badly, when you discover they were in an unsafe situation, or when they make a choice that breaks your heart. As moms we blame ourselves for not being able to discern their every need, for working too much and seeing them too little, for being on the phone when we should be in their faces, and for not knowing the latest when it comes to what might be in their food—or in the air—that is now linked to causing cancer.

We blame ourselves, feel the guilt, and believe we are solely responsible for how they turn out.

Kelly, a young mom (who, in my opinion, has it together far more than many moms I've observed) worries about how she is raising her only son, three-year-old Dexter.

"Since I'm a natural worrywart, I have many concerns. I worry that he will pick up our bad habits. I worry that we could be doing more to help him be successful in the future and be all that God intended him to be. I worry about whether or not we are building a good foundation for him to develop a relationship with God that he can depend on.

"I also worry about how he treats others and if he is learning respect. I worry that his happy spirit might diminish. I worry that we are too hard on him or provide too much pressure, and that we give in to his demands too often. I worry too about what effect it will have on him with all grandparents, cousins, and immediate family living long distance from us, and about the type of environment he is growing up in and how different that is from my and my husband's childhood experience. I worry about the food we eat and how all the new additives and sugars might affect his development and his ability to learn.

"As he approaches grade school, I worry about the exposure to peer pressure and what questions he might come home with; playing sports and the competitiveness even at young ages; affording the type of schooling best for my child to learn and reach his full potential; and managing a school schedule with both working parents. I also worry about our ability to steer his interests in the right direction and give him the best opportunities to explore, making sure there is time to be a kid and play.

"I worry about navigating what he sees and hears in the world. Obviously, we go out, get on planes, go to malls, and visit other people, but once he goes off to school he'll be exposed to different values."

Sometimes Kelly even worries about what Dexter worries about—his fears at noises in the middle of the night, his thought that bad guys might enter the house while they're sleeping, and so on. And sometimes she's worried that her concerns are causing *him* to worry.

"Many times he can sense when I am upset or worried, which I worry that I shouldn't project in front of him."

Oh the cycle of fear, worry, and guilt that we put ourselves through!

The Weight on Our Shoulders

According to a 2014 Barna Group report, the average woman who is a mom is stressed because of all she believes she should be able to do:

> There is a new reality for women in the 21st century—it's a different world with different goals than it was even a generation ago. As little girls, today's women didn't grow up with only dolls and toy kitchens and princesses and visions of idyllic domesticity and motherhood behind a white picket fence. They were given these, but also given a little plastic doctor's bag and a coloring book full of potential careers to choose from.

> "You can be anything you want, child." It's a message of empowerment and it's beautiful. But, as many of those young girls grew up, a message that was once meant to convey opportunity has begun to feel like a pressure cooker. What once was "You can have it all" has now become "You need to have it all." You need to have the perfect job, the perfect husband, the perfect house, the

perfect kids, the perfect play dates and craft nights and date nights and do-it-yourself Pinterest projects and #nofilter Instagrams.[2]

We are told we can have it all. And we *want* to have it all. And we want to *do* it all, provide it all, and get it all right. As my friend Stephanie Shott says in her book, *The Making of a Mom*: "It's pretty hard to be all and do all when you're really just overwhelmed by it all."[3]

We place such heavy expectations on ourselves that we end up becoming stressed-out moms carrying unbearable loads. And yet God never expected us to live that way. He never put any expectation on us to do it all. He meant for us to depend on Him to do the heavy lifting. That's why He put commands before us like…

- "Be still, and know that I am God" (Psalm 46:10).

- "Cast your cares on the LORD and he will sustain you" (Psalm 55:22).

- "Come to me, all you who are weary and burdened, and I will give you rest" (Matthew 11:28).

- "Take my yoke upon you and learn from me…For my yoke is easy and my burden is light" (Matthew 11:29-30).

- "Be anxious for nothing, but in everything by prayer… let your requests be made known to God" (Philippians 4:6 NASB).

God wants to do a work in you and me as we rely on Him for help with a task that, at times, seems daunting.

The Root of Our Insecurities

There are a number of factors that can contribute to our parenting insecurities and make us moms who worry.

How We Were Raised

Many moms I interviewed for this book were insecure about their mothering abilities because of how they were raised. For example, Kadee, a young military wife stationed in Japan with three young girls, says she prays for the assurance that she's doing "a good job."

"I didn't have godly parents and my husband didn't either, so we don't really know what we are doing when it comes to raising godly children," Kadee said. "I just hope and pray that we are doing good by our children and they are being well taken care of."

Do you ever look at what you didn't have and wonder if it's causing a deficit in your children's lives too? If you had a mom who never spent much time with you, it might be second nature for you to keep to yourself and your work and not spend much time with your own child. Or if you experienced very little communication with your mom, it might be difficult for you to talk with your child on a deeper level. If you were verbally or physically abused, you might be afraid that those negatives will surface in your own parenting (we will explore this further in chapter 6). In whatever way you were raised, you might feel that it impacts your ability to be a good mom.

Our Children's Needs

We also tend to feel unsure about our mothering abilities because of certain needs our children have. Maybe you have a child with special needs, or you gave birth to a set of twins when you weren't expecting any more children, or you have a child with a temperament similar to or unlike your own. Maybe you've adopted a child with deep-seated insecurities and abandonment issues that you aren't sure now how to deal with. Maybe you have a child with ADHD or food allergies or some other condition that requires an inordinate amount of attention that you wonder at times if you can even give. Those situations, and others like them, can make any mom feel intimidated and discouraged.

How Our Children Are Behaving

We can also doubt our ability to parent by the way our children behave. Unfortunately, *none* of our kids behave as instructed 100 percent of the time. All children have minds of their own and will, at times, do the strangest, stupidest, grossest things. And as we stare on in horror all we can do is gasp...or pray. See if you can't relate to some of these worries or concerns, all of which I have heard *numerous* times, by the way, over the past 20 years of ministering to moms:

"I can't understand a word he says. How will he ever succeed in school?"

"He eats every wretched thing he finds on the ground. How will he ever live past four years old?"

"He can't keep his fingers out of his nose. And he can't keep those boogers out of his mouth!"

"I don't know where she heard that word. She certainly didn't learn it at home!"

"I never imagined she would do such a thing. I did not raise her that way."

"I can't believe she got another tattoo!"

"All I have to do is breathe and I embarrass them. What gives?"

"I never thought I would be saying that about my own child."

"Who would've thought my child would _____?" (Maybe by now you can fill in the blank with your own unexpected reality.)

If your child seems out of control right now, you may be feeling as though you are unqualified for what is to come in the days ahead.

What Others Are Saying

Sometimes we end up worrying about our inadequacies—or questioning our parenting abilities—based on what others say to or about us. Jamie, a mom of six children (three of her own and three she inherited from her husband), says, "I continually tell moms, especially new ones, that there is no one way to be a good mom. All moms are different and all children are different. If there was a single right way, everyone would be doing it. It's easy to feel guilty and beat yourself up as a parent. All you can do is pray, read Scripture, and make the best decisions you can."

God Understands Your Concerns

When it comes to how you were raised, your children's needs, and the seemingly difficult task before you (whether you're caring for an infant, toddler, child, teenager, or young adult), I'm sure you've heard well-meaning people say that God gave you that child "because He knew you could handle it."

I won't suggest, however, that God "knew you could handle it" and that's why He gave you the kids you have. That would imply there is something intrinsically great in you and me that enables us to be amazing moms. I will venture, instead, to say, "God knew you wouldn't be able to raise your children without Him," so He put those kids in your care (and made you the mom that you are) so you would lean in close to Him and depend on Him every step of the way.

That, my friend, is the first secret to becoming a worry-free mom: entering into a day-to-day reliance on the One who knows all things and through whom you can do all things (Philippians 4:13).

The Source of Our Confidence

We all have some sort of baggage or dysfunction in our past. (Think about it—what family is truly 100 percent *functional*?) And all of our children, to some degree, have special needs or require additional time, or have their bad behavioral moments (no matter how old they are!). The reality of life is that you and I, and our children too, are broken individuals who will experience temptation, make the wrong decisions, endure a season of rebellion, and so on. But here's your confidence: God not only selected you to be your children's mom (whether through birth or adoption), but He knows exactly what you struggle with in relation to what type of child or children He's given you. And He has a way of even orchestrating the circumstances you and your child go through so you will learn to partner with Him to get through this journey.

All through the Bible, we read stories of how God chose seemingly incapable individuals to accomplish great tasks, and we can be encouraged to know God can do the same in our lives.

For example, there is Moses—that Hebrew baby who was set adrift on the Nile River so he wouldn't be slaughtered by the Egyptians, and was rescued by Pharaoh's daughter to grow up as royalty in the palace. He was chosen to be God's deliverer of the Hebrew nation. But it wasn't because he was educated in Egypt and had close ties to the Pharaoh. God chose Moses *after* he had been away from Egypt for 40 years, herding sheep and getting to know God a little better. In fact, Moses claimed to be "slow of speech" (which may mean he stuttered or didn't speak well in public), and yet God made *him* to be His mouthpiece to the intimidating Pharaoh of Egypt.

Moses was no Toastmasters' graduate. He wasn't a guy fully confident in his abilities. That's probably why God chose him. In fact, Scripture calls Moses "more humble than anyone else on the face of the earth" (in the King James Version he's called "very meek").[4] Now, if I were going to assign someone the task of delivering hundreds of thousands of people out of the hands of a powerful and oppressive nation, I wouldn't exactly pick the meekest person I knew. Yet God wanted someone who would *fully depend on Him* for the task at hand. God wanted someone who would readily admit the power was not his own, but came from God. God wanted an incapable human for a superhuman task. So He chose a weak vessel into which He could pour His vast strength.

I believe God wants to do the same with you and me. I believe He wants you to fully depend on Him as you raise that strong-willed, high-need, attention-deficit, tantrum-throwing, or nerve-wracking child in your home.

Yet there are certainly times we wonder if even God realized what He was doing when He made us moms.

Seasons of Doubt

Kadee felt the heaviness of the question "What did I do wrong?" when her second daughter, Lily, was two years old and diagnosed with "failure to thrive."

Little Lily wasn't gaining weight as rapidly as she should have for her age, according to a chart used by medical professionals that determined optimal height and weight at various ages.

"I feel like a horrible mom," Kadee told me in a text when she received the news. But Kadee wasn't a horrible mom. She had two little girls, thirteen months apart, and the older one was a voracious eater and the younger one wasn't. Lily wasn't complaining about not getting enough food. She certainly wasn't starving. She just wasn't keeping up with a specific growth chart. And because Lily wasn't making a fuss about it, wasn't sick, and apparently wasn't starving, her "condition" pretty much went unnoticed.

The doctor prescribed a special diet and close monitoring of how much Lily was eating. The family drastically altered their meal-time routine to make sure Lily was eating the proper amount of the proper types of food. Within a month, Lily was gaining weight appropriately and the pressure lessened with each month that followed. Kadee now has a third child and told me recently that when little Eliza turned two, she was also diagnosed with "failure to thrive" and Kadee was told to go through the same routine all over again.

I've heard that same story repeatedly—a common situation in the babies' developmental years that is easily remedied and yet moms carry guilt about it, not realizing many other babies also go through the same "disinterest in eating" phase.

Stages of Life

Many of our insecurities about parenting surface because we find ourselves in a situation that is new or different. As a result, we feel as if we're in a circumstance no one else has encountered or will understand. But Scripture tells us in Ecclesiastes 1:9 that there is nothing new under the sun.

During my daughter's early teenage years, I remember saying—out of frustration—"I don't know how to do this. I've never parented a teenager before!" (Now that must have been real comforting for her to hear, don't you think? To have a mom who admits she's clueless. Either that, or it made her feel she had some sort of edge over me.) That was the day I went into my study, closed the door behind me, got down on the floor, and called upon God—the Perfect Parent—who has gone before me into every stage of life my daughter will live through, and every stage of parenting I will experience. That's when I went to *the God who knows the future* for help one day at a time.

Raising our children is all about helping them navigate the changes and stages of life. But those changes and stages can throw us for a loop at times and cause us to question our abilities or effectiveness as a parent. Thankfully we have a God who knows exactly what's coming, will walk with us through the circumstance, and reminds us that this too will pass.

In Ecclesiastes 3:1 we are told, "There is a time for everything, and a season for every activity under the heavens." The next seven verses list "a time to be born and a time to die, a time to plant and a time to uproot, a time to kill and a time to heal, a time to tear down and a time to build," and so on.

We will look more closely at that passage in chapter 4, at which time I will share insights on how to preserve your sanity during your children's different stages in life. But for now, I want to encourage your heart with this: There will be times when you doubt your abilities as a mom, and times you feel very confident. There will be times you are failing miserably, and times when you get it right. The important thing to remember is that through all that you face, you have an Unchanging God who will be a steady, immovable rock you can cling to when things start swirling around you.

Trust His Faithfulness

As your children go through varying stages of temper tantrums, bad attitudes, feeling embarrassed at your presence, unexplained irritability, moodiness, and hormonal changes, remember this one thing: You have a God who never changes. His ear is always bent toward your voice. His arms are always available for you to run into. His words of wisdom are always there for your benefit.

Usually when change occurs we become uncomfortable because a situation is unexpected or catches us unprepared. But if you think about it, our lives are all about change—changing jobs, changing houses, changing neighborhoods, changing churches, changing computers (as you upgrade and learn a whole new system), changing phones (and losing all your contacts). And oh, how the changes can sometimes make you feel as though you're going crazy! Unless you are firmly grounded in the One who never changes.

Scripture says God is the same from age to age. He "does not change like shifting shadows" (James 1:17). He is an immovable rock. And His wisdom, compassion, and stability are there for us when we absolutely don't know what to do.

So although there is a time to weep and a time to laugh, He is there to comfort us when we need solace. And although there is a time to mourn and a time to dance, He is there to grieve with us and celebrate with us as well. And although there is a time to scatter stones and a time to gather them, He is there giving us the wisdom to know which season is which and how we are to get through them.

I'm so thankful that Ecclesiastes 3:1-8 does not include "a time to receive God's help; and a time to depend on your own devices." Rather, *every* season is a time in which we are to look to God for His help.

Scripture reassures us in all 26 verses of Psalm 136 that God's "lovingkindness is everlasting" (NASB). That means His character will never change. Unlike your child, God will never go through a stage in which He feels moody, unmotivated, indifferent, temperamental, or unwilling to help you. Because God doesn't go through stages, you can depend on Him to be a steady anchor when everything around you is changing and has you feeling panicked.

God always knows what He's doing in our children's lives. And get this: He always knows what He's doing in *your* life as well. So let this God of Stability help you be as stable of a mom as possible through all the changes in your children's lives. I guarantee that, if you haven't already, you'll be asking yourself repeatedly, "Am I getting this right?" But you and I don't have to ask that question anymore. We don't have to wonder if we have the right formula, the right set of rules, the right advice, the right personality, or the right responses. We have the right God. He's powerful. He knows all things. And He gives wisdom, generously, to anyone who asks Him for it (James 1:5). So by looking to Him and His Word, we can gain all the help we need. And we can lose all reason for worry.

Your Next Step

In the introduction of this book I had you start with the ABCs: (1) **A**dmit you are not in control; (2) **B**elieve God wants only the best for you and your child; and (3) **C**ommit yourself to a deeper knowledge of God. Your next step is to follow the instructions in Philippians 4:6-7:

> Don't worry about anything; instead, pray about everything. Tell God what you need, and thank him for all he has done. Then you will experience God's peace, which exceeds anything we can understand. His peace will guard your hearts and minds as you live in Christ Jesus (NLT).

To worry about nothing and instead pray about everything is easier said than done. You might be wondering: *How do I find the time to pray? And how do I know if I'm praying enough? How do I remember to pray about everything? How do I not get discouraged if I pray and nothing seems to happen? And besides, sometimes it's hard to pray.*

You're right. Sometimes praying *is* difficult. But probably not for the reasons you think. It's not because you don't say the right words or have the right techniques or set aside the perfect place to pray. Our heavenly Father tells us that when we are in relationship with Him we can come boldly and confidently—at any time—and ask Him for what it is we need and be assured that He hears us (1 John 5:14-15). Yet there is an enemy of our souls who doesn't want us praying. He wants to distract us, discourage us, and make us believe that our prayers are ineffective and a waste of time.

And yet prayer is one of the most effective things you can do for your child. It certainly carries more weight—and productivity—than worrying. God wants us to talk to Him about our children, our concerns, and our hopes and dreams for them. It's the way we open the door and let Him into the daily decisions—and anxieties—of parenting.

Author Robert Jeffress makes two observations about prayer: (1) you will always struggle with prayer; and (2) you don't have to be good at prayer to be effective.

Jeffress explains that Paul used the term "strive with me in prayer" when he wrote to the Christians in Rome (see Romans 15:30) because prayer was, indeed, a struggle. "When we pray we are, first of all, wrestling with an enemy who is bent on our destruction," Jeffress says.[5]

Satan knows how effective our prayers are. As James 5:16 says, "The prayer of a righteous person is powerful and effective." Satan knows how much the living, all-powerful God bends His ear to listen to the requests of His own and therefore he will do anything he can to distract you, discourage you, or delay you from praying. He will cause you to want to give up before you start. Or to feel overwhelmed and think, *There's so much to pray for I don't know where to start*, or *God knows what I'm going to say anyway, so I'll just let Him read my mind.* (I know, that's a pathetic cop-out—one that I've used multiple times myself, in fact.) And of course, Satan harasses us with this thought: *You're no good at praying, so don't think God will even listen to you.*

I guarantee you will find it difficult to set aside concentrated times to pray, to have the confidence to pray, to know what to pray about and to wonder if you're praying well enough or correctly. But that's where the beauty of Jeffress's second point comes in: *You don't have to be good at prayer to be effective.*

Jeffress cites, in his book *I Want More!*, the example of Paul and Silas in prison. They had asked the Roman Christians to pray for their release. Apparently the Christians had prayed, but evidently they weren't convinced their prayers would have any effect. God caused an earthquake in the vicinity of the jail, and Paul and Silas escaped. When they came to the door of the place where the small group was praying for their release, the group wouldn't even let the men in. They didn't believe it was them! How's that for a lack of faith and power in prayer?

And yet God released those two men...despite the lack of faith, lack of zeal, and lack of hope exhibited by those who were praying.[6]

That is so encouraging to me. That tells me that you and I have hope too. That when we utter, "Please help me, Jesus," He will. That when we say, "I don't know what to do with this child; please intervene!," He will. And when we are at our wit's end and full of grief because of choices a child has made, He absolutely hears and gives us the peace that no one else could. God's response might not come the way you expect, but He will take your prayer and do something with it.

If you're starting to think, *But I've already tried praying and it didn't accomplish much,* or *I'm not very good at praying,* be assured of this: Prayer not only changes much, it changes us.

According to Philippians 4:6-7, prayer is what brings peace to our hearts. Even though God already knows what you're going to say, He wants you to pray because of the peace that accompanies your heart, mind, and soul once you've been in His presence. How loving of Him—God doesn't want us to miss the beautiful, restful, calming experience of communing with Him.

Becoming Active in Prayer

Here's a process which spells out the word P-R-A-Y that you can begin incorporating into your life right now to start gaining the peace you need as a parent:

P—Pray to Commune with God, Not to Get What You Want

Are you in a state of continually talking with God, or do you pray only when things have gone wrong or you need help? As you develop a daily communication with God, you will come to trust Him as easily as you breathe. Trust will be a part of you, like a close friend. And worry—that deep, fearful anxiety of what might be—will soon be a stranger who no longer pesters you.

That's what you want—the kind of everyday relationship in which communication with and trust in God is the most familiar friend to you and worry becomes a distant stranger.

R—Reach Out for Help

Rebecca, a mom of two young daughters (whom you'll hear more from in the next chapter) says, "Like most moms I know, I feel like a deer in the headlights half the time, wondering, *What's the right response or plan or consequence?* But I am unbelievably blessed by the other Christian wives and mothers in my church who are willing to reach back and help a sister in need—sharing God's truth, no matter what, letting me know I am not alone. Satan wants us isolated and insecure; God wants us in the glowing light of a community of women who have been there and are willing to share what He has taught them." And Kadee, whom we met earlier in this chapter, said the instruction and wisdom of other moms has helped her tremendously: "I am a first-generation Christian in my family, other than my great grandparents, so I've had a lot of self-learning to do as a Christian parent. But God is faithful and has provided me with the right leaders and friends to help me do right by my children."

Do you have a community of mentor moms who can help you (and to whom you can minister as well)? If not, here are some suggestions:

- If your kids are preschoolers, find a MOPS or similar moms group at a Bible-teaching church in your community. These groups are full of encouragement, support, and practical help.

- Become a part of The Laundry Moms community (www.thelaundrymoms.com). This is an online community of encouragement and support for moms. You'll find helpful articles, daily reminders of what matters, and a host of loving, experienced moms who are available for you. You can also find The Laundry Moms on Facebook and Twitter.

- Learn more about the M.O.M. Initiative (M.O.M. stands for Mothers on a Mission to Mentor Other Mothers). This organization, started by my friend Stephanie Shott, provides biblical resources and support that give mentors and small-group leaders the confidence, courage, and community they need to connect with other moms.[7]

- Are you a single mom? Check out SMORE (Single Moms Overjoyed, Rejuvenated, & Empowered!), an alliance of compassionate women whose goal is to encourage single moms to reach their full potential. This dynamic group of caring women based in Texas get together yearly for retreats that offer some tender loving mom time with other women who understand the pressures and concerns faced by single moms.[8]

- Finally, get articles, advice, daily encouragement, and meet other moms like you who are taking the "Worry-Free Challenge" at my Facebook page: Worry-Free Moms.

A—Ask God for Wisdom, Not Necessarily the Answers

Oswald Chambers wrote, "Spiritual lust causes me to demand an answer from God, instead of seeking God Himself who gives the answer...Whenever we insist that God should give us an answer to prayer we are off track. The purpose of prayer is that we get a hold of God, not of the answer."[9]

I've learned to daily seek God for wisdom so I can have His mind, not my own. It's like consulting that Voice within that knows better than you do how to handle and respond to parent-child issues and concerns.

Y—Yearn for a Closer Walk with God

I am convinced that every relationship we care about, every area in which we hope to succeed, everything that means anything to us comes down to how closely connected we are with God. As we learn to love God, we are empowered to love others. As we serve Him, we are enabled to serve others. As we value His opinion of us over others, we are able to better and more maturely relate to our kids, especially as they get older. As you long to know God more, to please Him in every respect, it will show in your parenting.

But most of all, as you lean in closer to God and look at what His Word says about who He is and what He's capable of, you will live with confidence rather than fear. And you will find yourself becoming a worry-free, wisdom-filled woman and mom.

Partnering with God

I hope you are ready to drop your guilt and insecurities and recognize that you are part of a team in which the primary parenting is coming from Someone who never gets it wrong. Parenting, after all, is a partnership. Whether we admit it or not, the sovereign God of the universe knows what your children's future holds. He knows what your children will become, how they will contribute to this world, and more. Don't you want to be a part of that exciting journey? Partner with Him now...it's never too late. And He will carry you through the days—and years—ahead.

Putting It into Practice

A Prayer for Partnering with God

God, thank You for giving me the child(ren) that You did. Thank You for assigning me this task, knowing full well I would need You to get me through it. I surrender to You my insecurities, my confusion, my weaknesses, and even the things I think I am really good at, knowing You will exchange them all for Your confidence, Your wisdom, and Your strength. I surrender to You—not with an "I'll do my part, You do Yours" mentality, but "I surrender to Your complete control." Forgive me for my desire for control, which results in my worry. Help me to remember that in everything, You are God over all. And no matter what You decide to do from here on out—in my life and in my children's—I trust You. Let the adventure begin.

Becoming a Worry-Free Mom
—in Community

For Thought or Discussion: In what areas of parenting have you most wondered, *Am I doing this right?*

1. Read the following verses and record any insights you gain about how God can encourage or help you as a mom:

   Psalm 22:19— He's not far he's my strength.

   Psalm 25:4-5— He's my teacher + my guide.

   Psalm 31:3— He's my rock!

   Psalm 121:2-3— He won't let me fall. He's got me!

   Proverbs 3:5-6— TRUST in him

   Philippians 4:6-7— DONT worry PRAY

   1 John 5:14-15— I can ask God anything

2. Who can you reach out to who has gone before you in the parenting journey? How will you reach out to her or them this week?

3. Read James 5:17. In what area(s) do you need to ask God for wisdom?

   Trust

4. What is one thing you can do, starting today, to lean in closer to God?

   Pray and ask him to replace worry with his thoughts.

2

Be Careful

....

Secret 2: Realizing God Can Control
What You Can't

*B*ecky never guessed that the much-anticipated summer gathering at her home for Jacob and his friends would turn out to be the most crucial and defining point of Jacob's life—and clearly the scariest moment of hers.

Becky's 17-year-old son Jacob had invited a group of his friends and his football team to his country home for a day of outdoor fun that was to culminate in a bonfire and the firing of a cannon that he and his friends had made. Jacob's family had applied for and received all the necessary permits for the activity. Twenty teenagers and five adults were present, all having a great time until Jacob tamped the cannon and it misfired.

The gunpowder blew into Jacob's face, chest, right arm, and hand. He was thrown backward and into the air by the force of the blast before landing facedown.

"We all thought he was dead because he was lying so still," Becky recalled.

"He suddenly jerked up and took a breath like the first breath of a newborn. There was fire on his chest, so his sister pulled his shirt off of him and the soldiers that were in our group poured water over his head because his face was covered with powder burns and his eyes were swollen, black, and burning."

Jacob was flown by helicopter to a burn unit, where he was admitted and treatment began. He was unable to see anything, and his right eye was severely damaged. The family was told that the powder burns would be "easy" to deal with, but the medical professionals had no idea whether or not he would regain his sight.

I will let Becky describe for you how she was feeling during that horrifying time: "I was *worried.* Jacob is excessively afraid of the dark. We were concerned he would be in darkness for the rest of his life. We thought his dreams for the future would be stopped cold. We wondered if he would be permanently disfigured.

"I was *stressed.* We did not have any health insurance at the time, and treatment in the burn unit cost six thousand dollars a day. We were in a city away from home during his stay. My husband and I both had to take time off of work to be with him.

"I was *fearful*—for Jacob's life, his emotional well-being, his eyesight, and his faith in God…that it might waver during this time."

Yet despite Becky's fears and concerns, neither Jacob, nor his family, were alone or without hope during this ordeal.

"Enter God!" Becky said, and described the turn of events that followed.

"From the moment of the blast, God interjected Himself into the situation. The force of the blast had caused Jacob to stop breathing, which, we found out later, had kept burnt powder from entering his lungs and causing more severe problems. Upon discovering that, we felt a peace that came from figuring that God was working His plan through all of this. Dear friends brought us clothing and pillows, and offered their homes for rest and to take showers.

"Most of all, we noticed the absence of any anger or bitterness in our seventeen-year-old son. Jacob was pleasant and friendly to the staff and to the many visitors who came and encouraged him. This is actually his normal self, but we wondered if his condition would take a toll on him and cause him to be irritable. He remained hopeful around others, but during the night, he would ask me, "Mom, what if I never see again...?"

"When we left the hospital, his right eye was drooping and had that 'blind blue' look to it. He wore dark glasses when out of the house and could not see anything from his right eye. His left eye was not strong, so his perception was off."

And yet God knew what He was doing in Jacob's life and heart... and in the hearts of everyone in his family.

"God took that blind eye and healed it completely within two months' time," Becky said. "Almost daily, we noticed improvement. When he first could see through it, he saw no colors. Then he was gradually able to distinguish colors and details. He went back to school with corrective lenses. By the time he was released by the ophthalmologist, his vision was 20/20 in both eyes! His vision had originally been 20/13.

"Jacob has a few scars from the powder burns that won't go away... they are constant reminders to us of God's goodness, provision, and peace, and a testimony of what He has done in Jacob's life to all who see and ask about them."

Jacob's accident would make any mom shudder. Yet what the family originally considered an accident they now see as part of God's divine plan to show His love and mercy to all of them. They all got an up-close and personal experience with God, experienced His hand of protection over them through the ordeal, and saw His ability to redeem that situation into something beautiful.

Was Becky worried during the ordeal? Absolutely. But God clearly knew what He was doing—and He knows what He's doing in *your* child's life and your family too.

Their Unseen Protector

Usually we assume that if our children encounter danger, it won't be at our own house. Rather, it'll happen somewhere else, or when they're off doing something they shouldn't be. Yet as Becky discovered, dangerous situations can occur right under our noses—reminding us that we are not in as much control of our children's lives and surroundings as we would like to think.

That's why we trust in our Unseen Protector, who has every situation under control whether we think it's safe, or we are suddenly hit by danger.

"She'll Be Fine"

My husband, Hugh, has never liked hearing me say to Dana, "Be careful."

"She'll be fine," he would always respond after my warnings. Several times he explained to me that he didn't want our daughter to grow up timid or fearful of trying new things.

And several times I explained to Hugh that it's natural for a mom to caution her child and be concerned about a child's well-being.

When Dana was about four or five years old, we took her to the Muir Woods National Monument near San Francisco. Dana was trying to keep up with two boys of similar age who were running on logs, climbing up and jumping off of rocks, and having a grand adventure.

We were having a great day, except...each time Dana climbed up and ran across a mossy (read: slippery) log, I would yell: "Be careful, Dana."

By the third or fourth warning, Hugh had just about had it. "*Stop* worrying about her, Cindi. She's *not* going to fall and get hurt!"

"You don't *know* that, Hugh," I responded, a little agitated by now that he continued to reprimand me for being a cautious mom. "She could very easily fall and get hurt. I just want her to slow down so that won't happen."

"She'll be fine," Hugh responded, this time with more agitation in his voice about having to say it again.

And as soon as those words left his mouth we heard the shriek. We turned just in time to see Dana slip from a log, fall through the air a few feet, and then roll about 15 feet down a grassy, wooded slope.

My rescue instincts kicked in and as I bolted toward her, I feared the worst. I envisioned a few broken ribs, abrasions and cuts from the rocks, and—even worse—a concussion from the fall.

I reached her first, relieved to see that she appeared relatively unscathed. She was whimpering, apparently shaken up by the fall. I could tell she was fighting back tears so as not to cry in front of the boys she had been trying to keep up with.

Hugh arrived just behind me and said, "What a *great* fall, Dana! And that was an *awesome* roll. And look, you're not even hurt!" At that, she grinned, regained her confidence, shook off the dirt from her clothes, and started back up the hill to join the boys.

"See?" I said to Hugh. "That's *exactly* why I was telling her to be careful!"

"And see?" Hugh retorted back. "She didn't get hurt, did she? She's *fine!*"

To this day, I realize Hugh could easily have been wrong about his whole "she'll be fine" theory. Dana could've hit her head on a rock when she fell, or damaged an eye from picking up a twig on her roll down that hill. But she didn't. And I was thanking God the rest of the afternoon that she was protected from my worst fears during that scary-looking fall.

That day, I was reminded once again that our children are in God's hands. And whether they get hurt or not, He is there to cushion their fall and get them back on their feet again.

She's Doing What?

Chery recalls worrying about her daughter during two situations that looked extremely dangerous.

"Our daughter, Chrystal, is a talented equestrian," Chery said. "She was just born with it. I have taken more heat from family and friends for encouraging her in such a dangerous career path. She is also good with children and people cannot understand why I don't encourage that instead. I was always firm in my conviction that God gave her this gift and He expected us to support her in developing it. But I started to question that myself when she was about twelve. She loved to 'live' at the ranch about a mile from us. She took lessons there and her trainer was quick to pick up on her talent. So she started letting Chrystal hang out after her lesson and taught her how to grain the horses and do other jobs. Then her trainer asked if she could come help out on Saturdays. So I would drop her off at nine in the morning, and when I picked her up at five in the afternoon, she would be so disappointed and say, 'Why are you here so soon?'

"One day when I came to get her there was a lot of hubbub. Everyone was going to the arena. I asked, 'What's going on?' One of the boarders said, 'You've got to see! Chrystal is riding Esprit!'

"Esprit is a horse *no one* rode except the trainer. This horse was dangerous, strong-willed, and unpredictable. I suddenly froze in fear. I felt my heart jump into my throat, followed by a wave of nausea, followed by anger toward her trainer, followed by a plea to God to keep her safe. I worked my way to the front of the crowd and watched as I saw the most beautifully fluid union of horse and rider galloping around the ring. God's peace washed over me. I looked at Chrystal's face and could see she was 'gone'—completely unaware of her surroundings, fully immersed in her relationship with Esprit. Watching my daughter on that horse was like watching art in motion.

"I walked away thanking God for the gift of what I saw, for *her* gift, and for giving me His peace. I knew that would not be her last ride on Esprit. Nor would it be the last time she was in a dangerous situation. So that specific prayer of thanks to God became part of my prayer life as I continued to trust God for her safety around her horse work.

"About three weeks later, when I went to pick up Chrystal, I walked into the barn aisle and heard a great deal of thrashing around. I passed her trainer and said, 'What's happening?' She said a horse was having a bad day and she sent Chrystal to deal with it. I came around the corner to hear Chrystal say in a loud, firm tone I had not heard before, 'Knock it off—I'm not afraid of you! Whoa!' In the stall, all I could see was this large horse reared up and snorting as it pedaled its front legs in the air, an outstretched hand, another outstretched hand with a riding crop, and the top of Chrystal's head. The flush ran up my chest into my face and my eyes welled with tears. My heart raced so fast I could feel and hear the pounding of it in my ears. Fear had gripped me and I couldn't speak. My mind ran to my heavenly Father; He flooded me with His peace and trust once again, and gave me Psalm 46:10: 'Be still, and know that I am God.'

"The horse settled, I heard Chrystal pat her several times and say 'Good girl…that's a good girl.' Then she opened the stall door and said, 'Hi Mom! Have you met Tiny?'"

Fearing the Worst

Chrystal's horse stories turned out to be great examples of a mother's unfounded fears. But I know what you're thinking. What about those times when God doesn't still the horse? Or cushion a rider's fall? Or restore a person's eyesight? What about when He appears *not* to protect?

I used the word *appears* because God's Word tells us that He is good and kind and cannot act apart from His nature. He is a perfect Father who knows how to care for His children. But there are times when we who live in the physical realm can't see what God is doing in the spiritual realm to protect our children. We may not realize that, although He let a child fall and get hurt, He is working toward an even better good in their life than if it had never happened. What God does is sometimes beyond our ability to fathom. But then, we aren't God. And that's when our trust in Him is essential.

There is statistical evidence that most of the things moms worry about—like sudden infant death syndrome (SIDS), a missing child, or a fatal catastrophe—rarely happen.[10] But you might be thinking, *What if my child is the exception? What if my child is the one who dies early, is kidnapped, or is seriously injured?*

When it comes to your child's well-being, chances are *something* will happen (if it hasn't already) that will rock your stability and scare you. That's the nature of the world we live in. And we need to realize God will allow things to happen to our children that make them—and us—utterly dependent on Him.

For me, it happened when Dana was 18 months old.

A Defining Moment in Our Lives

One day as I put Dana down for a nap, I was a little concerned about a couple of bruises on her legs and one on her arm. But she was a toddler, and toddlers often stumble and fall and bump into things, right?

But after she woke up, I saw a large bruise on Dana's forehead. And then I *knew* something was wrong.

I called her pediatrician and described the situation. He said, "I need to see Dana immediately."

The pediatrician took a blood test and sent me home with instructions to wait by the phone. As soon as we arrived, he called.

He informed us that Dana's blood platelet count was dangerously low and that was why she was bruising so easily. He ordered us to take her immediately to Loma Linda University Children's Hospital and plan to stay there with her for at least the weekend and possibly into the next week. There she would see the best blood specialist in the country and take a bone marrow test.

"Whatever you do, make sure she doesn't bump her head on the way to the hospital," he added. "It could cause bleeding on her brain and she could go into a coma."

I put down the phone, packed quickly, and we left for the children's hospital, which was about an hour and a half from our home. While my husband drove, I was silent—with two things running through my mind: (1) I had worked for a newspaper and written several articles about bone marrow donors and transplants and I knew that bone marrow problems were usually associated with cancer or leukemia; and (2) all my life I'd learned that God was in absolute control of all things, so I knew this did not take Him by surprise. I couldn't help but feel this was the defining point of whether I really trusted God or if I just *talked* like I did.

Dana was assigned to the pediatric oncology ward—a whole floor of toddlers to 12-year-olds lying in beds or pushing around chemo carts. Little bald girls and boys everywhere. It was the saddest thing I have ever seen. Dana was the youngest patient admitted to the floor at that time.

Dana and I stayed in her room Thursday, Friday, and Saturday nights, where nurses came in every couple of hours through the day and night to draw blood from Dana's little veins and check the level of her blood platelets and then hook her up to another intravenous blood glucose injection to raise the level of her platelets so she could recover. The nurses informed us the doctor would be arriving Sunday afternoon and order a bone marrow test for Monday morning.

Hugh planned to take the day off from work on Monday and be there with me, along with a few friends who also promised to come be with me when the staff would insert a needle into Dana's spine and draw marrow from her bone to see if she had leukemia or cancer.

Sunday morning, while Hugh was back at our little church preparing to preach his sermon in another half hour, the nurse came into our room and announced, "The doctor just arrived. He wants to do the bone marrow test *now.*"

My first thought was, *My support system isn't here. They don't even know back at church to be praying right now...they all think this is going to happen tomorrow.* I was ushered down the hall with Dana, all the while praying, *Oh dear Jesus, please be with her and me...because we're all alone right now.*

Because Dana was a baby, the medical team had no intention of using anesthesia, and the thought of that needle going into her back and drawing material out of her bones just horrified me. (They wouldn't do it to an adult without anesthesia, yet they'd do it on a baby and let her feel every bit of it!)

As I was holding Dana and praying, she fell asleep in my arms. The nurse took her from me gently, went into the room, and closed the door behind her.

I sunk down onto the floor on the other side of the door and prayed, *God, this did not take You by surprise. You know exactly what's going on in her little body. You already know the results of that test. Make your presence powerful right now, in that room, and right here with me. I know I am not alone...and Dana isn't either. And thank You for arranging that this test be taken earlier than we expected so You could be the One to sit here with me.*

As I sat on the floor praying, I waited for the scream and the crying to come from behind the door, but it never came.

Dana slept through the entire procedure—through the needle insertion and the bone marrow pull—all of which requires the patient to be kept strapped down and motionless throughout. She was still asleep when they handed her back to me 25 minutes later.

The next morning, the doctor informed me that the lab was analyzing the results of her test and we could expect to know the results in about a week. He also said the blood glucose injections had been working and her platelet level was high enough for her to go home. They fitted her in a little padded helmet to protect her head and she was released from the hospital three days earlier than expected.

A week later, we reported to a specialist, who informed us that the bone marrow test results were negative for cancer or leukemia, and that Dana's blood platelet level had not dropped since she'd been home from the hospital. We were told that she most likely had a rare condition called ITP, in which the body attacks its own blood platelets for unknown reasons. He said the average child recovers anywhere from six months to five years. But in some cases, it's a chronic condition that comes and goes throughout their lives.

We returned to the doctor another week later, and were told her blood platelet level still hadn't dropped, but had actually increased a little. We came back to the doctor a third time three weeks after her release from the hospital. Her platelet level had continued to increase, and we no longer needed to see him. The doctor told me, "I have never seen a child recover so quickly and thoroughly from this disease."[11]

My Path Toward Peace

I don't call Dana's medical scare a nightmare. In fact, I refer to it today as my path toward peace—the defining moment in which God built my confidence in Him. And I am actually grateful for that scare for a number of reasons. First, it reminded me, as a young mom, that I am not, nor have I ever been, in control of my daughter's health, life, or destiny. Second, it taught me where true peace is found. Not in pleasant circumstances. Not in the feeling that "all is well in her world." But in the palm of God's hand as He allows whatever He will to come her way and mine. And finally, it gave me an experience to look back on and build my confidence upon whenever I begin to worry, doubt, or fear for an event in Dana's life—or my own.

God showed me through Dana's brief hospitalization that He has been there for her (and me) before, and He will be there for her (and me) again. I'm very grateful for that lesson early on in Dana's life—and in my parenting—that nothing happens outside of God's knowledge or control. I've also learned that, as a parent, nothing is more important than trusting God every step of the way...even through the dark when I can't see the outcome. In fact, *especially* during those times.

Gaining Perspective

We live in a world that can get downright scary at times. Accidents happen. Evil appears to triumph every now and then. And we can find ourselves debilitated by fear as we focus on the "what ifs" and imagine the worst. After all, at any instant, life could spin out of control. But there is a calming truth and anchor of hope in this uncertain world. And that is this: We never were in control anyway. God always was and always will be. Nothing takes Him by surprise. Though something might catch you completely off guard, God knew it was coming and was prepared to get you and your child through it. He's ready to calm your worry, steady your hand, and steer you to the next stage of His plan.

I realize that as I say that, you might be feeling a little uneasy. I don't think we'll ever completely relax when we consider the dangers that might come our child's way. That, in essence, is why we worry. But in doing so we are fearing the odds, the worst, the things that might happen in a world that turns at random. But that's not the whole picture. You and I live in a world with a sovereign God who controls every aspect of it.

At this point, you might be thinking, *If God is in complete control of everything, why doesn't He just prevent these types of things from happening in the first place? Then I would never need to worry at all!* From your perspective and mine, that would appear to be the solution. But God has chosen not to eliminate dangerous situations from our lives, but rather to teach us how to trust Him in spite of and within the dangers of this world so that we have a greater understanding of His love, provision, and purposes.

God is going to allow what He's determined to allow (Isaiah 46:9-10). But we have a wonderful promise in Romans 8:28-29 that what He allows is for the good of those who love Him:

> We know that in all things God works for the good of those who love him, who have been called according to his purpose. For those God foreknew he also predestined to be conformed to the image of his Son.

That passage assures us that *in all things* (even what you and I consider accidents or close calls) God is working for the good of those who love Him and are called according to His purpose *so that* we can be conformed to the image of His Son. *So that* your child can get to know or depend more on God. *So that* you can experience a closer walk with and reliance upon God. *So that* others can look at what God has done or how He has worked good in it and praise Him for it.

That verse tells us clearly that God is working on our eternal good—the shaping of our character, the molding of our being into the image of Christ. Consider the fact that bad things happen in this world whether you know God or not. But wouldn't you want your child to be right in the palm of His hand and you be experiencing

His unfathomable peace when those things happen? Rather than struggling against circumstances you can't control and stressing yourself—and your child—out? As you and I look at the good that God has worked in the lives of the people who share their stories in this book, we will come to realize that yes, we can live with full confidence that no matter what happens, God is in complete control and there is no better place to be than in His hands.

Making Sense of Our Children's Pain

It is natural for us to want to spare our children from suffering. Yet suffering is the tool God often uses to bring our children into a saving knowledge of Him or a more intimate relationship with Him. It's also what He uses to bring us moms into a stronger dependence upon Him.

Remember how Becky quickly recalled the goodness of God in spite of Jacob's accident? Not only did God change her son's heart through it, but the priorities, perspectives, and prayer life of her entire family changed through that event as well.

I absolutely understand if you cringe at the thought of seeing your children endure anything that will be uncomfortable or painful for them. Yet we don't have the ability to shape our children for eternity, to instill in them traits like compassion, gratitude, a maturity beyond their years, a perspective that they are on this Earth for a purpose, and a faith in God that is tried and tested. Only God can do those things. And He often accomplishes them not by keeping our children completely safe, but by showing Himself strong in situations in which they might suffer. God may want to work on some character traits or deep-seated values in your child's life—or yours— by permitting something you consider "unsafe."

When God chooses to allow your child into a situation you don't think is "safe," you can be assured that He knows what He's doing and He has His eye on the outcome, on the life-changing, eternal benefits that can come from "unsafe" situations. He is either teaching you or your child how to pray more fervently, remember His presence, or recognize His ability to provide and protect.

In both Jacob's and Dana's lives, God came through and showed Himself strong on their behalf. And today, those two young adults know that they lived through a situation that should have taken their lives, their eyesight, their vitality. Yet they are still here. How that gives them confidence that they are here for a reason! How that gives them a story to share with others about Him and His ways. How that helps them to know they have a God who loves and protects them.

Now those are gifts Becky and I could never have given to our children. They are gifts that come only through experiencing God's loving hand in the face of danger.

Dealing with the What Ifs

Most of our worries involve the question "What if…?" Fears of what might be are a result of our minds spinning out of control as we ponder possible negative scenarios. But rather than focusing on the terror of what might be, we need to focus on the truth of what is. To continually ask "What if…?" is to deny that God is in control.

In Philippians 4:6-7 we are told, "Do not be anxious about anything, but in every situation, by prayer and petition, with thanksgiving, present your requests to God. And the peace of God, which transcends all understanding, will guard your hearts and your minds in Christ Jesus."

In the New Living Translation that verse reads:

> Don't worry about anything; instead, pray about everything. Tell God what you need, and thank him for all he has done. Then you will experience God's peace, which exceeds anything we can understand. His peace will guard your hearts and minds as you live in Christ Jesus.

I don't think it's a coincidence that the next two verses tell us how to think:

> And now...one final thing. *Fix your thoughts on what is true*, and honorable, and right, and pure, and lovely, and admirable. Think about things that are excellent and worthy of praise...Then the God of peace will be with you (verses 8-9).

Here's a perfect example of why we shouldn't pick a verse or two out of a paragraph to read or memorize and then stop reading. These *four* verses in context all work together as instructions for us to not worry and *how* to not worry. God is giving us the complete formula for how we can eliminate worry and experience His peace:

Step 1: Don't worry about anything. (It's a choice. Choose not to worry.)

Step 2: Pray about everything. (It's a command. Just do it.)

Step 3: Fix your thoughts on what is true, honorable, right, pure, lovely and admirable...excellent things, worthy of praise. (God is very specific about what we are to "fix" our minds on so we aren't held captive by negative, fearful thoughts.)

Step 4: Experience God's peace. (As a result of the above three steps, God's presence will be with you.)

Do you realize that most of our anxiety and worry comes because we are *not* taking the last two steps in that four-step process? We are failing to fix our thoughts on what is true and honorable and right and pure and lovely. Instead, we fix our thoughts on the negative possibilities, the worst that could happen, the scary "What if...?" scenarios. The Bible clearly tells us that is *not* the route to peace.

To fix your thoughts on what is true is to focus on the reality of a situation, not the possibility or supposed danger. And fixing your thoughts on what is honorable, pure, lovely, admirable, excellent, and worthy of praise is to focus on God and His character.

I've given you a chart to help you see how to focus on what is true when your child is in a situation that might otherwise cause you fear.

What Is True:	What Is Feared:
Your child is with a friend for the day.	Your child is engaging in something dangerous/inappropriate.
You haven't had a "check-in" call from your teenager.	He cannot call because he's lying on the road injured or dead.
Your daughter is not home and it is past curfew.	She is in a helpless, intimidating, dangerous, or foolish situation.
Your child has a cough, fever, or infection.	His condition is worse than it appears and he will not recover.

Some of the fears listed in the right column might seem a bit dramatic. But isn't that what happens sometimes? When we encounter a situation, it doesn't take long for our minds to get to the worst-case scenario, does it? That's what worry produces—a fear that the worst may have happened.

This next chart summarizes the above situations and how they produce irrational fears when we aren't focused on what is true about God and the situation. Look at it closely.

What Is True:	What Is Feared:
You are not in control of a situation.	God is not in control, not aware of the situation, or not good.

Now, I know you wouldn't speak those thoughts aloud or admit that is your train of thought. Yet your worry speaks those words for you. When you and I worry, we are saying to God: "I don't believe You are powerful over this situation. I don't trust You to work it out. I believe I'm on my own." In fact, I once heard a pastor say "All worry assumes God doesn't know, He doesn't care, or He doesn't have the resources."

Now let's reverse that chart to summarize your fear and show you how to *replace* that fear with what is true:

What Is Feared:	What Is True:
Nobody (including you) knows where your child is.	God is aware of every detail (Psalm 139).
You—or your child—are not prepared to handle a situation.	Nothing takes God by surprise; He is able (Ephesians 3:20).
Your child is alone and helpless.	God has promised to never leave him (Hebrews 13:5).
Something "bad" may happen.	God causes all things—even what you fear—to work for good to those who love Him (Romans 8:28).

One way to replace worries with the truth is to focus on the reality of God and His character. In other words, the truth is that God is good, loving, kind, compassionate, all-knowing, and all-powerful.

To focus on what is true and right and good and pure is not simply a matter of positive thinking, nor is it a case of naive wishful thinking. It is a practice of *placing your trust in a good and loving God and the positive things He is able to do in your life and the life of your child.* It is the practice of saying each day, "You, God, are in control, and I'm not. And that's okay, because You know better than me. I don't know what's going on, but You do, and I thank You for that." It is an exercise in faith.

Faith is not merely "a belief in God." Rather, faith is a lifestyle. Hebrews 11:1 defines faith as "the assurance of things hoped for [and we hope for the good things, not the bad things that might happen] and the conviction of things not seen [the conviction that God really is working behind the scenes even if we can't see it or imagine how He will work it for good]."

So, faith is having a deep assurance of the good things we hope for, as if God has already accomplished them. Faith is being convinced that God is working behind the scenes for our good, even when we can't see or imagine it.

What if you had that kind of confidence each time your child was running a fever, or not home on time? When it comes to such scenarios, God wants you to know Him deeper and trust Him in a way that you never have before. And to turn your children over to Him and trust that they're in loving, capable hands is one of the most practical ways to show God that you trust Him with your whole heart. He wants you to experience that kind of peace—a peace that is made possible by the Unshakable, Immovable, Ever-Stable God.

Whispers of His Love

God asks us to trust Him unswervingly in a world in which bad things still happen. But He doesn't just tell us "trust Me" and then check out until we've passed the trust test. He gives us little—and big—reminders every day that He sees, He hears, and He is working in ways we might not have noticed.

Rebecca, a mom of two girls, ages ten and seven, experienced what she calls "every parents' nightmare." But she also knows the peace of God as never before, and she is convinced that God is in complete control over her life and the lives of her children.

"We had a terrible situation with our youngest daughter a few years ago. Just suffice it to say, we were unable to prevent every parents' nightmare. But I felt God's presence surrounding me immediately, like I had never experienced Him before. In the days that followed, I felt like the Lord was holding us and protecting us, even with the craziness that was swirling around us." Rebecca said there is a specific passage of Scripture that has been pivotal in helping her family to keep the right perspective:

> Rejoice always, pray continually, give thanks in all circumstances; for this is God's will for you in Christ Jesus (1 Thessalonians 5:16-18).

"This verse helps remind me that every moment is an opportunity for me to thank God for the lessons He's teaching *me*, and that His plan for my family is so much more than whatever circumstance we find ourselves in, no matter how awful it may be.

"Giving thanks for God's hand in our minor annoyances or our terrible situations helps us turn our hearts back to Him and acknowledge that His plan is greater than ours. It makes us remember that He is working on our behalf.

"If we can keep bringing our minds and hearts back in alignment with Him, even though we falter, we learn more and walk straighter with each new opportunity for growth through trusting His plan for us that we cannot see."

What About You?

Wow! Can you and I trust God like that regardless of what our children go through? I know it's much easier said than done. But if a mom who has experienced "every parents' nightmare" can keep her peace knowing that God is in full control, so can you...

- when you leave your child in someone else's care
- when your child has symptoms and you're waiting for a diagnosis
- when your daughter goes on her first date
- when your teenager takes the car out for the first—or fiftieth—time
- when your college freshman attends a school far from home
- when your child ventures out to another country
- when it's been days, weeks, or even months since you've heard from your child

Developing that kind of trust in God isn't easy. But it's inevitable when you get to know this God who can control what you can't. By leaning into Him and learning more about His character, you will find yourself gaining the peace and assurance that your child is much better off in His hands without you anywhere around, than if you were standing right there with your child and you both were on your own.

You can start right now to practice this truth by replacing the words "Be careful" with the words "Be in His care." Because your child *is* in His care...whether you remember it or not.

Putting It into Practice
Trusting God with Your Fears

Here are three steps to living out Philippians 4:6-9 and praying about your worries so you can replace them with God's peace—right now.

Step 1: Worry about nothing

In the space below write out two or three of the worries that cause you to tell your child or children, "Be careful":

That harm will come to them

That they'll make bad choices

Step 2: Pray about everything

Now, take each of those worries you've written above and give them to God in prayer. I've provided a template below that can help get you started. Fill in the blank with your worry and say this prayer as many times as you need to with the blanks filled in with as many worries as need to be prayed about. As you complete that prayer for each worry, draw a line through what you wrote above. You have handed that worry to God, and it is now in His hands.

> God, Thank You that You know all about my concern
> for _____(child's name)_____ and _____
> _____(insert your worrisome situation here)_____.
> I realize this situation has not taken You by surprise, and
> You are already working in it for my child's good and my
> good too. Thank You that You are more interested in
> building eternal benefits and godly characteristics into

me and my child than You are about assuring me that
he/she is "safe." I trust You, and I invite Your peace to
replace the worry in my life.

Step 3: Fix your thoughts on what is true

Now it's time to redirect your thoughts from the "what if" scenarios to what is true, right, pure, lovely, and good. We do that by
focusing on God and His characteristics. In the space below, make
your own list of what is true about God by writing down ten things
you know to be true of God's character. (I completed the first few
for you.)

Ten Things I Know to Be True About God

- He has promised to never leave those who trust in Him
  (Hebrews 13:5).

- There's nowhere my child will go where God will not follow (Psalm 139:7-12).

- God's ways are perfect (Psalm 18:30).

- You know the very fiber of their being

- You know the plan! (future)

- Nothing can seperate her from Gods love.

- All things work together for good!

- They are first his.

- God has entrusted them to me! (he trusts me)

- He's slow to anger abounding in love.

He is patient.

He pursues us!

Step 4: Embrace His peace

The next time you find yourself thinking a worrisome thought or saying, "Be careful," follow those thoughts or words with a quick missile prayer to the Only One who really can keep your child in perfect care. Here are seven missile prayers you can choose from—or, write one of your own on the line below:

Hold him tightly—he's in Your care.

Guard her carefully—she's Yours.

God, keep them in Your hands and keep me in perfect peace.

Lord, You are in control—remind me of that moment by moment.

Lord, this situation didn't take You by surprise. Grow me and my child through it.

God, You are in control, and I'm not. And that's okay, because You know better than me.

I don't know what's going on, but You do, God, and I thank You for that.

_____

Becoming a Worry-Free Mom —in Community

For Thought or Discussion: Think about an "unsafe" situation that your child made it through, or a situation in which you worried he/she wasn't safe. What actually happened, and how does the outcome increase your trust in the God who watches over them?

1. Maybe you've experienced some close calls with your children. If so, list those close calls here and what you learned about how God came through for you and your child:

Your Child's Close Call:	God's Deliverance:

2. Read each of the following passages of Scripture and indicate if that verse is for your comfort, or something you will pray over your child. Then circle the one(s) that you want to memorize or write out as a frequent reminder that helps you not worry about your child's situation.

Psalm 27:1— *The Lord is my light + my salvation. whom shall I fear*

Psalm 32:7— *You are my hiding place protect me from trouble.*

Psalm 46:1— *Ever present help!*

Psalm 55:22— *Cast your cares on him.*

Psalm 56:3-4— *When I am afraid I put my trust in you.*

Psalm 62:1-2,8— *You have heard me!*

3. Complete a chart of your own similar to the one on page 54, listing your own fears or worries on the left

side and writing down the truth—about God and that
situation—on the right side.

What Is Feared:	What Is True (About God):

Why This?

My friend, Midge, felt heartsick the day her only child was diagnosed with alopecia—loss of hair for unknown reasons.

Her four-year-old daughter, Ellie, had been losing hair in one small patch on the front part of her head. And Midge was shocked when the doctor informed her that her daughter might go bald within the next year or so, and furthermore, might wrestle with keeping hair on her head her entire life.

Midge is an elementary school principal and aware of how kids can be ostracized or made fun of if they are different in some way. So she was immediately concerned about how Ellie would fare in school. She enrolled Ellie in preschool, hoping to encourage her social skills and confidence in making friends before losing most of her hair. Midge also sought medical treatments for Ellie to prevent further hair loss, and joined a support group for parents of children with alopecia.

Mostly, though, she worried.

What if she is a social outcast?

What is she is the subject of ridicule at school?

What if she never has a boyfriend because of this?

Maybe we should invest in long-term wigs.

By second grade, Ellie had nearly a full head of hair. But by sixth grade she had lost a lot of it again. There was a pattern. Her hair would fall out in the fall when it got colder, and grow back in the spring.

"Ellie had a strict teacher in fifth grade and her hair fell out more. I realized then that her condition was also stress-related," Midge said.

Ellie never went completely bald. Her hair would come and go and, at its worst, she lost 75 percent of it in patches mostly toward the back of her head. However, the hair loss didn't seem to bother Ellie as much as it did her mom.

"In my mind, I thought, *She looks like a very ill little girl,*" Midge said. "I thought, long term, no man will ever want her. Looking back, I realize I didn't trust the Lord would take care of her. I obsessed over her condition. I worried day and night over it. I couldn't tell my husband how I was feeling. I internalized it."

Ellie's alopecia became more manageable through the years, and today it worries neither her nor her mom. Midge now looks back on those years and sees that she was a worried mom with a situation that God had under complete control.

"I'm embarrassed now that I hadn't trusted God about it," Midge said. "And now, I feel that because I had her later in life and she was the only child I had, I could've focused a lot more on her looks had this not happened."

Because of Ellie's hair loss, Midge says, "We emphasized her intellect and how she treated others. In hindsight we emphasized the things that really mattered and she grew up very confident and very compassionate of others. It saved us a lot of girl drama in the end."

God's Purposes

When Ellie was diagnosed, Midge had asked God and others, "Why this?" Yet God knew exactly what He was doing—He was shaping Ellie's character, as well as her mom's.

"Beauty fades anyway," Midge says. "And Ellie developed a heart when we couldn't put much emphasis on her hair! I wish I'd had faith that God would restore her hair, but also I know now that there was a lesson to be learned, a different path she was to take."

Ellie is now 22 years old with a full head of hair that falls nicely over the four or five small gaps on the back of her head. She is also one of the most compassionate, authentic, and nonmaterialistic young ladies I know. Recently she donated 12 inches of her hair to Pantene's Beautiful Lengths, which makes wigs and provides them, free of charge, to children who have lost their hair due to chemotherapy or other medical treatments.

"Ellie finally got that full head of hair she's been wanting for years, and she celebrated by cutting it off and donating it so someone else can celebrate having a full head of hair," Midge said.

Although Midge originally asked, "Why this?" it's clear to her now that God took what she and her daughter thought was beautiful—long hair—and replaced it with something that truly *is* beautiful—a loving heart.

When We Can't See It

Every mom encounters a situation with her child in which she asks, "Why this?"

Why this, God? She was such a beautiful little girl.

Why this, God? He finally raised his grades and started acting responsibly.

Why this, God? Haven't my children been through enough already?

Why this, God? She is just a child.

Yet God has His purposes and I probably don't need to tell you this by now, but...they are higher and better and so much grander than ours.

In Isaiah 55:8-11, God gave us insight into how His perspective often differs from ours. And as you read this, think about the situations in your children's lives in which you have asked, "Why this?"

> "For My thoughts are not your thoughts,
>   nor are your ways My ways," declares the LORD.
> "For as the heavens are higher than the earth,
>   so are My ways higher than your ways
>   and My thoughts than your thoughts.
> "For as the rain and the snow come down from
>   heaven, and do not return there without watering
>   the earth and making it bear and sprout,
>   and furnishing seed to the sower and bread to the
>   eater; so will My word be which goes forth from My
>   mouth; it will not return to Me empty,
>   without accomplishing what I desire,
>   and without succeeding in the matter for which
>   I sent it" (NASB).

Now read the next two verses, in a different Bible translation. Imagine this as our response when we realize that God knew all along what He was doing in the lives of our children while we were asking, "Why this?"

> So you'll go out in joy,
>   you'll be led into a whole and complete life.

The mountains and hills will lead the parade,
  bursting with song.
All the trees of the forest will join the procession,
  exuberant with applause.
No more thistles, but giant sequoias,
  no more thornbushes, but stately pines—
Monuments to me, to God,
  living and lasting evidence of God (verses 12-13 MSG).

If you and I can hold onto those burning questions during the confusion and apparent silence of God, then we too can be "bursting with song" in the parade of praise to God—"exuberant with applause" at what we saw Him do in the life of our child...and in our own heart as well.

Angel's Story

Kim Eaton remembers asking "Why this?" on a day that her life—and her daughter's—changed for good.

On October 23, 2013, Kim received news that no mom ever wants to hear. Her only child, 15-year-old Angel, was diagnosed with Ewing's sarcoma, a rare type of bone and soft tissue cancer.

"Instead of worrying about boys and curfews, all of a sudden I found myself wondering if my daughter was going to die," Kim said.

Within a few days of being admitted to Children's Hospital of Birmingham, Angel underwent two surgeries. The first was a bone marrow biopsy and aspirate and the surgeon drained nearly two liters of fluid from her lung. In the second surgery, doctors placed her port and did a tissue biopsy. Her chemotherapy treatments started just nine days after her diagnosis.

The road wasn't easy. Kim and her daughter were in survival mode. Get through this. Beat the disease. Remain optimistic. Trust God.

"Over the course of fourteen months, Angel had twenty-six rounds of chemotherapy, six weeks of radiation (thirty treatments), and surgery to remove her tumor along with three left ribs. Angel spent more than half of that time in the hospital for chemotherapy, fevers, and infections. She went into anaphylactic shock because of an allergy to some random antinausea medicine. She ended up in Special Care several times for low blood pressure and in the ICU once for the same reason. She was even airlifted (probably one of the scariest moments of my life). And then, when we were nearing the end of her treatment, we had a huge scare. Her oncologist saw something unusual in some of the scans they do every so often and thought the cancer might have spread to her spinal cord. Needless to say, I have never prayed so hard in my life.

"The biggest worry, of course, was that my daughter wouldn't win this fight," Kim said. "It hurt so much to see her in pain, and I couldn't fix her or take the pain away. And of course I was stressed over finances," Kim said.

As a single mom, she had only her income and didn't have money saved to cover the cost of a catastrophic illness.

"During Angel's treatments, I was still trying to work so I would have a job to come back to and so I would be able to keep up with my house payment and monthly bills."

During all this, Kim's heart went out not only to her daughter, but also to many others whom they met over the course of Angel's treatment. "We grew close to many families whose children had cancer, and they were constantly on my mind and in my heart," Kim said.

And—as you will see in the other stories throughout this book— God came through.

A little over a year later, Angel was declared cancer-free. She finished her last chemo treatment on December 1, 2014, and the doctors pronounced her NED (no evidence of disease) a month later.

"Angel will continue to have follow-up scans and tests every three months, and then every six months for quite a while. But the cancer is gone," Kim said.

We Don't Have to Be Supermom

Kim admits she wasn't supermom upon hearing of Angel's diagnosis and helping her through all her treatments. And even though Kim was raised in a Christian home with a solid biblical foundation, she wasn't superspiritual mom either. She didn't immediately have complete peace and think, *Well, nothing takes God by surprise, so here we go.*

No. She was scared for her child's life, as any mother would be.

"When I first learned of Angel's diagnosis, I had every emotion under the sun coursing through my body at various moments. I was scared out of my mind, frustrated, and angry that God *allowed* something like this to happen."

Well-meaning family and friends tried to encourage her, but their attempts backfired.

"I got tired of people telling me that God has a purpose and plan for everything; I seriously could not figure out what purpose He had for allowing a fifteen-year-old girl to get cancer," Kim said.

"Then one night, I just lost it. I broke down and bawled my eyes out for hours. I questioned, I yelled, I totally freaked out—and then this crazy, insane calm came over me and the only thing I could think was this: *You're scared, and that's totally understandable, but it's not your job to question. It's your job to trust and have faith.*

"That doesn't mean I was calm for the next fourteen months. I still had moments of doubt and weakness. But when it really mattered, I could feel God's presence."

God's Provision

Although there were unanswered questions and continued frustrations, Kim's experience of God's provision for her—and her daughter—was an encouragement to her.

"For every worry I had, God provided," Kim said. "Every time I received a bill in the mail and didn't have the money to pay for it, we would get a donation from someone within a couple of days.

"For every scare or test that my daughter had, my devotional reading for that day provided the exact scripture and words that I needed at the time. For example, the day we went in for Angel's scans and were about to learn that she was cancer-free, my morning devotion began like this:

> I am able to do far beyond all that you ask or imagine.
> Come to Me with positive expectations, knowing that
> there is no limit to what I can accomplish.[12]

"The scripture that accompanied the devotion was Isaiah 40:30-31 (one of my favorites during this time): 'Even the youths shall faint and be weary, and the young men shall utterly fall, but those who wait on the LORD shall renew their strength; they shall mount up with wings like eagles, they shall run and not be weary, they shall walk and not faint.'

"The next morning, this was my daily devotion: 'It is impossible to praise or thank Me too much.' The scripture that followed was 'Praise the LORD! Praise the LORD, O my soul. I will praise the LORD all my life; I will sing praise to my God as long as I live' (Psalm 146:1-2).[13]

"God's timing was always perfect in providing for me, whether or not I realized it in that moment," Kim said. Kim's comfort and reassurance that God was in control wasn't found solely in a devotional book, but in the Scripture verses contained therein.

We are told in Hebrews 4:12, "The word of God is alive and active. Sharper than any double-edged sword, it penetrates even to dividing soul and spirit, joints and marrow; it judges the thoughts and attitudes of the heart."

The fact that God could make His Word penetrate Kim's heart and be completely applicable to her circumstances on the very day that she read it is one of the many ways that Scripture is "alive and active."

Furthermore, 2 Timothy 3:16-17 tells us, "All Scripture is God-breathed and is useful for teaching, rebuking, correcting and training in righteousness, so that the servant of God may be thoroughly equipped for every good work." Kim found the "breath of God" for what her soul needed on specific days.

As we saw earlier, Isaiah 55:10-11 says that God's Word will not return to Him empty, but will accomplish what He desires and achieve the purpose for which He sent it. Kim saw firsthand how God's Word—a little each day—did not return empty. It gave the comfort and assurance she needed at just the right time.

When You're Tempted to Worry

In Matthew 6:25-34, Jesus instructed His followers to not be anxious or worrisome about the everyday details of life—where they'd get their next meal, what they would wear, and so on. He told them to look around and notice how God fed the birds of the air and clothed the lilies of the field. And He would take care of them even more because they were so much more valuable to Him:

> Look at the birds. They don't plant or harvest or store food in barns, for your heavenly Father feeds them. And aren't you far more valuable to him than they are?...And if God cares so wonderfully for wildflowers that are here today and thrown into the fire tomorrow, he will

certainly care for you. Why do you have so little faith? (Matthew 6:26,30 NLT).

And then Jesus drove home His point by saying, "Seek first his kingdom and his righteousness, and all these things will be given to you as well. Therefore do not worry about tomorrow, for tomorrow will worry about itself. Each day has enough trouble of its own" (verses 33-34).

I love how those last two verses in that passage are translated in The Message. They encourage us to look at the bigger picture—what God is doing in what we can't immediately see:

> Steep your life in God-reality, God-initiative, God-provisions. Don't worry about missing out. You'll find all your everyday human concerns will be met. Give your entire attention to what God is doing right now, and don't get worked up about what may or may not happen tomorrow. God will help you deal with whatever hard things come up when the time comes" (Matthew 6:33-34 MSG).

Did you catch that? Give your entire attention to what God is doing *right now*, and don't get worked up about what may or may not happen tomorrow. That advice should keep any of us from worrying when we're tempted to ask, cry, or plead, "Why this?"

Kim offers this advice to moms who tend to worry about the small stuff: "Enjoy the time you've been given with your family and your friends, and don't let the little things in life take away your joy and peace. Don't worry about the things you have no control over because it's a waste of time. I know it's much easier said than done, and I was definitely one of those moms before my daughter was diagnosed, but my perspective on life has definitely changed."

And when it comes to bigger life-threatening things?

"Trust in God with all your heart," Kim said. "He has a plan and His timing is perfect. You might feel like you and God are in different time zones, but He knows what He's doing."

There it is again: *He knows what He's doing.* It's a recurring theme in the life of a mom concerned about her child, for sure. And it's another one of those secrets that leads to a worry-free life—having the assurance that God knows exactly what He's doing.

The "Mother Heart" of God

When Jesus talked about God in relation to those who were trusting Him, He identified Him as our heavenly Father. Jesus also told many parables so that we would more clearly understand our relationship with our heavenly Father. But did you know Scripture also contains passages that help us understand God's "mother heart" as well?

I believe God wanted us, as moms, to know how very much He cares for us *and* our children, and that He can relate to our hearts—and our concerns for them—not just as a father, but as a mother too. In Isaiah 49:15, God says:

> Can a mother forget the baby at her breast
> and have no compassion on the child she has borne?
> Though she may forget,
> I will not forget you!

And in Isaiah 40:11, the prophet Isaiah said this about our God who cares for moms and their children:

> He tends his flock like a shepherd:
> He gathers the lambs in his arms
> and carries them close to his heart;
> he gently leads those that have young.

We have a heavenly Father who cares about the intimate details of our lives. And it's not just life-threatening cancer cases that God is tuned in to. He cares just as much about our struggles with allergies, acne, and alopecia. He cares about weight problems and skin conditions and situations we believe might negatively affect our children or their chances of living normal, happy lives.

What Only God Knows

Although Kim would never have wished cancer on her daughter under any circumstance, she can confidently—and honestly—say that she wouldn't trade that experience for anything. It changed her daughter's character in an amazing way, and it has brought the two of them closer together.

"Both Angel and I have grown so much closer to each other and, more importantly, to God during all of this. We've witnessed miracles over and over, met some amazing and inspiring people (including hundreds of young cancer patients and their families), and learned the importance of not taking life for granted."

Through all that happened, Kim witnessed her daughter's transformation into a teenager who values life and fights for causes she believes in. Instead of spending her weekends hanging around at shopping malls, Angel is organizing rallies and events to raise awareness for and fight the disease of cancer.

Angel has a Facebook page called Angel's Warriors and through it she rallies prayer warriors to join her in the fight against cancer—not just on her behalf, but also on behalf of the many others she meets who are fighting the disease as well.

Trusting His Best

How many times do you and I see a situation and want to change it, fix it, or rush in and rescue our children to spare them from any type of suffering? Yet God, the perfect Father, allows children to go through circumstances that will develop them into the kind of adults He wants them to become. And He allows moms to go through situations with their children to develop them into the women He desires they be. We're never too old to be shaped and molded into the likeness of Christ. And, as I mentioned in chapter 1, He will often give us *more* than we can handle so we will find it necessary to fully depend on Him.

"People told me all the time that the Lord doesn't give you more than you can handle," Kim said. "I disagree. I think He does because only then do you realize that you can't make it without Him. And why would you want to?"

I too have heard many moms try to encourage one another, or themselves, by saying "God won't give you more than you can handle." But that promise or assurance is not in the Bible. We are told that "God…will not allow you to be tempted beyond what you are able, but with the temptation will provide the way of escape also, so that you will be able to endure it" (1 Corinthians 10:13 NASB). But when it comes to struggles, there is no such assurance. To the contrary, God will allow us to experience more than we can handle so that we will depend on Him to handle it for us (Matthew 11:28-30). That is how we come to learn dependence on a God who can do through us what we cannot do alone. And that is how we learn to hide ourselves in Him (Psalm 32:7) and rest in His ability to shelter and protect us (Psalm 91:1-2).

Try This for Your "Why This?"

Kim didn't have a planned-out strategy for trusting God when Angel was diagnosed. At first she tried to handle matters on her own, which was what she had done for so long as a single mother. But the day she surrendered to Christ and placed her full trust in Him was the day she experienced peace. And now she recommends the following path to other moms who are dealing with worry and doubt:

1. Prioritize God's Word

Kim realized she had to counter her worries with the wisdom and comfort found in God's Word. So she committed to a daily time of seeking God and His life-building Word so that she wouldn't succumb to worry.

"My greatest source of comfort was definitely God's Word," Kim said. "My devotional time was the highlight of my day and God always provided the Scriptures that I needed exactly when I needed them."

Kim and Angel also clung to Philippians 4:13 throughout her fight against cancer: "I can do all things through Christ who strengthens me" (NKJV).

"It doesn't get much better than that," Kim said.

2. Pray Continually

"I also prayed—a lot," Kim said. "I would have conversations with God, not necessarily asking for anything. I had a lot of quiet time when Angel was in the hospital, and talking to God helped me get through those long days and nights without losing my mind (although I still ended up with a lot of gray hair!). First Thessalonians 5:17 tells us to 'pray continually.'"

Kim gives this advice: "Pray all the time, and understand that when you do, God might not answer your prayers the way you want. It's *His* will be done, not *your* will. But regardless of the outcome, you must continue to believe and have faith. I'm not saying it's easy. I've held the hands of several mothers who have had to bury a child… but you still have to believe that God will use even tragedy to bring someone closer to Him."

3. Praise God for the Good—and the Bad

"If He is worthy to be praised in the good times, why not in the bad times?" Kim said. "That is when you should praise Him even more; that is when your faith is being put to the test."

To praise God even when we're asking "Why this?" helps to change our perspective and reminds us that God truly is in control of all things. Scripture backs up Kim's suggestion. In 1 Thessalonians 5:18—right after we're told to pray continually—we are instructed to "give thanks in *all* circumstances [not just the good ones]; for this is God's will for you in Christ Jesus."

4. Pursue a Community of Support

Kim said, "Another huge source of comfort came in the form of texts, phone calls, messages, emails, and cards from friends, family, and random strangers. Each one held an encouraging word or prayer, love, and support, and they helped get me through each day."

In Ecclesiastes 4:9-12 we are told there is God-given strength in having others around us to sharpen us, encourage us, and hold us up when we begin to fall:

> Two are better than one,
>   because they have a good return for their labor:
> If either of them falls down,
>   one can help the other up.
> But pity anyone who falls
>   and has no one to help them up.
> Also, if two lie down together, they will keep warm.
>   But how can one keep warm alone?
> Though one may be overpowered,
>   two can defend themselves.
> A cord of three strands is not quickly broken.

Do you have someone you can look to for support when tragedy strikes? You were never meant to go through anything alone, especially as a mom.

Seeking the Answer

It's natural for us to want an answer when we ask, "Why this?" We want God to unfold His plan before us (so that we can let Him know whether we approve of it, I suppose). But God isn't going to do that. He wants your faith and trust. Faith believes God is good and capable without seeing where He is going with the situation. So instead of seeking answers to your "Why this?" questions, I encourage you to seek The Answer—that is, the Lord Jesus Christ, who holds your child's life, and yours, in His very capable hands.

Putting It into Practice
Trusting God's Unseen Work in Their Lives

1. Complete the chart below by writing, in the left column, all the "Why this?" questions you are asking in relation to your children. Then in the right column, list all the positives you can think of that are already coming out of the situation. If this exercise is difficult to do, pray that God will open your eyes to see His perspective on things. Think also about character traits and your child's long-term development. (Please don't skip over this step. Exercises like this are *crucial* to your understanding of how God works in our lives, and that understanding is what will give you peace in the days ahead.)

My Child's "Why This?" Situations:	How God Might Be Working:

2. In light of what you wrote above, praise God for what He is doing by writing out a thank-you note to Him in a one- or two-sentence prayer below. (Someday later, you might want to share this with your children to build their confidence and trust in how God worked—or is continuing to work—in their lives.)

Becoming a Worry-Free Mom —in Community

For Thought or Discussion: What has been your biggest "Why this?" that you've struggled with thus far?

1. Share with the group what you learned from completing the chart at the top of the page.

2. What do the following verses have to say about God's unseen work in your children's lives?

   Isaiah 55:8-11—

   Jeremiah 29:11-13—

   Romans 8:28-29—

   Philippians 1:6—

   Philippians 4:12-13—

3. Divide into groups of two or three. Pray for your own or each other's children, inserting their name(s) in the blanks:

   Lord, thank You that Your thoughts and ways are so much higher than mine and You know best when it comes to what _____ needs to one day be more like You. I trust that You will work for good whatever happens in _____'s life and that You will complete what You started in _____'s heart. Thank You that, as a mom, I can do all things through Christ, who gives me strength. Thank You that _____ can do all things through You as well. Make Yourself more real to us in every situation that we face. I trust You and Your glorious unseen work in our lives.

4

Will They Ever Get Through This Phase?

Secret 4: Relying on the Unchanging, Immovable God

*J*udy remembers when her teenage son wasn't motivated to do *anything*.

"He's very smart. And he's doing his work in class. He's just not turning it in. He forgets. Or he doesn't *feel* like making that extra effort to turn it in. I don't know what's wrong with him. It's so frustrating."

I had heard Judy's story before, but from Julie. And Mary. And Tina. And countless other moms. They sat across the table from me or in a small group with me or shared over the phone or through an email about their teenager's "lack of motivation" stage. Or their 12-year-old's season of mood swings. Or their 5-year-old's phase of testing the limits. None of these moms referred to their children's behavior as a season or stage or phase when they were venting their frustration, but that's exactly what it turned out to be. A temporary stage. A frustrating phase. A season that eventually ended.

In some cases, the phase lasted only a few months. In most cases, it lasted about a year. But in *every* case, it was a limited time, a bump in the road toward growth, a season of a child's life.

Judy summed it up beautifully when we had lunch recently. Now that her son is in his early twenties and quite responsible, she said, "I think most of the things we worry about come down to a phase our kids are going through. A phase that eventually ends and then our kid seems normal again.

"Every phase my kids went through, whether good or bad, seemed to change over time. I spent a lot of time worrying about something that wasn't even an issue a year later."

Blame It on a Stage

When I was a new mom, I was told by some well-meaning older moms and grandmoms that I could never blame my child's behavior on a "stage" that she was going through.

"Kids don't go through stages, they sin," I was told. "And therefore, their behavior is a result of their sin, not their stage."

Well, yes...and no.

The Bible says we're all sinners (parents *and* children), and we all fall short of the glory of God (Romans 3:23). Therefore, we need a Savior and the indwelling Holy Spirit to keep us from sin. And as we all go through stages of growing in the Christian life, we will go through stages of disobedience to God, stages of "testing the limits" with Him, and stages of dealing with the consequences of our sin as we learn to obey Him and walk closer to Him.

Mom, you have times in your life when you're not as happy or social as you normally tend to be. You have times when you're more melancholy, moody, and irritable. Just as the seasons of life bring about different moods and experiences and perspectives, so it is with your children. And perhaps even more so as they are growing and developing. In fact, their different stages can also amount to different stages of worry that we go through as moms.

While we need discernment to distinguish between what is a normal stage of life and what is a problem our children need help with, it is important to keep in mind that most of the changes our children go through—and the resulting worries—are temporary.

The Stages We All Go Through

God's Word speaks of normal stages and seasons of our lives. In chapter 1 we looked briefly at Ecclesiastes 3 and learned that no matter what happens in life, there is never a time that we are on our own or ineligible for God's help. Now I want to look at that passage again, this time a little more closely.

In Ecclesiastes 3:1-8, Solomon wrote this about the stages of life:

> For everything there is a season,
>> a time for every activity under heaven.
> A time to be born and a time to die.
>> A time to plant and a time to harvest.
> A time to kill and a time to heal.
>> A time to tear down and a time to build up.
> A time to cry and a time to laugh.
>> A time to grieve and a time to dance.
> A time to scatter stones and a time to gather stones.
>> A time to embrace and a time to turn away.
> A time to search and a time to quit searching.
>> A time to keep and a time to throw away.
> A time to tear and a time to mend.
>> A time to be quiet and a time to speak.
> A time to love and a time to hate.
>> A time for war and a time for peace (NLT).

Because this passage is a commentary on life, it can also serve as a commentary on a child's life. There will be times when your son is happy, laughing, so full of life. And there will be times when he is solemn, moody, and more contemplative than joyful. There will be times when your daughter is the life of the party and the shining star among all who know her, and there will be times she isn't as popular or enthusiastic. Let your children, regardless of their ages, go through the stages of life and learn from them. Ecclesiastes 7:3 says, "Sorrow is better than laughter, for when a face is sad a heart may be happy" (NASB). The growing-up experience includes many different phases—even those that are difficult for us to watch.

You and I can look at that passage in Ecclesiastes as a preview of parenting. And it also describes the different stages *you* will go through—as a woman, a mom, or a worrier (a *recovering* worrier, that is!).

Look at that passage again as it's translated in The Message (and note my paraphrasing in brackets to help you apply this to parenting):

> There's an opportune time to do things, a right time
>   for everything on the earth:
> A right time for [your child's] birth and another for
>   [your child's] death,
> A right time to plant [care for and invest in your
>   child's life] and another to reap [let them care for
>   you],
> A right time to kill [stop, delete, or let something
>   die] and another to heal [resume, restore, or
>   bring back],
> A right time to destroy [rebuke something] and
>   another to construct [build up something or
>   someone],
> A right time to cry and another to laugh,
> A right time to lament [grieve over your child's
>   behavior] and another to cheer [applaud and
>   encourage their behavior],
> A right time to make love [when they are married—
>   God's Word instructs] and another to abstain,
> A right time to embrace and another to part,
> A right time to search and another to count your
>   losses,

A right time to hold on [to your child] and another
    to let go [when they become older],

A right time to rip out [censor or keep things from
    them] and another to mend [give something
    back],

A right time to shut up and another to speak up
    [self-explanatory and so relevant for me!],

A right time to love [and support] and another to
    hate [some of the things they do or the unhealthy
    influences on their lives],

A right time to wage war [confront, rebuke, battle
    it out] and another to make peace [forgive and
    restore].

Did you notice what is missing in that list of seasons above? Scripture does *not* say there is "a right time to worry, and a right time to trust." That's because there is *never* an appropriate time to worry—only to trust that the God of the seasons and stages of life is sovereign over *this* season and *this* stage of your child's life as well.

A Time to Trust

There is never a right time for worry, fear, or doubt because worry is the equivalent of saying, "I don't think God can handle this."

One writer said, "Believe God is always the God you know Him to be when you are nearest to Him. Then think how unnecessary and disrespectful worry is!"[14] He also observed, "Nothing in our lives is a mere insignificant detail to God."[15]

Thus, there is never a time to mistrust God, to doubt He is working in the details of your child's life, or to fear that His plan is not the best for your child. You might be thinking, *I can recall several seasons of worry I've had in my life.* Perhaps, but God never intended for you to see that season as a time for worry, but rather, a time to trust.

Nancy's Season of Worry

Nancy recalls a season of worry in her life that paved the way to a time of trust. It all revolved around a stage her teenage daughter was going through.

"The most stressful time for me was when my daughter was around fourteen to fifteen years old, and the rest of her high school years, when she fell into some kind of self-awareness and depression," Nancy said. "It was very scary for me!"

Nancy didn't expect her daughter, Amanda, to fall into this depressed state, especially because Nancy had just married a year earlier, and Amanda, who had never had a father while growing up, finally had a dad.

However, when Amanda began high school and started hanging out with friends who dressed differently, Nancy began to worry. She witnessed her bubbly, social, outgoing daughter gradually become someone very different.

"Amanda became quiet and looked sad. Some say it was hormones as she was going through changes at that age. My husband and I continued to speak with her and do things with her, but she kept pulling away.

"She began wanting to hang out with her new friends by herself, and I wouldn't let her. I was a bit strict and would not let her go alone downtown to hang out with people I did not know. What I did know was that these other kids were all high school dropouts and tended to be a rough crowd, and I didn't think it was appropriate for my fourteen-year-old daughter to hang out with kids who didn't have any goals or aspirations or a relationship with God.

"But my husband believed I was too strict and that I should let Amanda hang out with her friends. He would say that she was a good girl and I had to trust God.

"After repeatedly objecting, I finally gave in to my husband's advice and let her go to town to hang out with her friends. I did not like it and it did not feel right! But I prayed a lot, asking God to watch over her. I made sure I dropped her off and picked her up and gave her time limits. Once I began letting her hang with her friends, she took advantage of that and would not listen, and things got worse. She became quiet, reclusive, depressed, and began cutting herself. I was confronted at a doctor's visit when they took her blood pressure (she was sick with a cold or flu) and saw the marks. I had no idea! It was the scariest moment for me. I felt naïve for not knowing. I did know that she was not her usual bubbly self because of the different way she was dressing, new friends at school (not her usual friends), but all else seemed okay. People kept telling me she was a typical rebellious child and it is a stage that all kids go through. I thought to myself: *I did not go through that dramatic of a change.*

"I talked to Amanda and asked her if there was anything she wanted to talk about and always told her that I was there for her no matter what and that I loved her and that God loves her. I took her to therapy too. We tried a therapist that our doctor's office recommended and then scheduled visits with someone at church. I continued to hear that this was a stage Amanda was going through and I needed to be patient.

"As time went on, I struggled and prayed a lot and prayed some more. Then I attended a church service in which the pastor spoke about worrying and said that it is a sin. My eyes opened up wide! I said to myself, *I am a big sinner, then, because I worry about my daughter all the time now!* It took about two years for me to really understand what it meant to not worry. I had always been one to attend church but I came to realize that I never really read the Bible. I continued to attend church and, as time went on, I learned to let things go and trust in God more. It was hard for me to let go of Amanda, especially because I struggled with feeling like I could have done more to protect her so she would not be depressed and going through all that she was experiencing.

"As time went by, things got a little easier—especially by still communicating with her, loving her, teaching her, and learning to let go a little more and trust more in God. I can't really say or remember a specific time when everything changed, but it was more of a gradual turn for both her and me to learn to trust and believe in the Lord. Amanda still has her struggles with being responsible, as any teenager does, but I have learned to take a step back and let her make her own mistakes so she can learn from them. I still watch out for her, but try not to control her.

"Peace came to me when I started to have a relationship with God and when I stood my ground with Amanda on certain convictions I had. I would explain to her my reasons and would explain to her that she too needs to trust in the Lord."

Amanda's depressed state *was* a stage. One she got through, primarily as her mom learned to trust God through the changes.

Surviving the Winds of Change

Here are some practical ways to stay sane during the various changes and stages your child will go through. These steps should also help you find your stability as well so that you can trust the God who has it all under control:

1. Learn to Respond Rather than React

Dr. Kevin Lehman, in his book *Have a New Kid by Friday,* says, "Often we react instead of respond. Our emotions get the better of us, and we speak or act without thinking first." This can escalate a situation between a parent and child, especially if you are reacting emotionally to something you don't understand (like your child's choice of dress or an unusual request).

Lehman explains the difference between responding and reacting: "If the doctor says, 'You responded to your medication,' that's good. If the doctor says, 'You reacted to your medication,' that's bad."

According to Lehman, reacting is answering emotionally and with the first thing that comes to your mind, rather than carefully thinking through the situation. Instead of reacting to something your child might say from a bad attitude or an irrational thought, respond by saying, "Tell me more about that."[16]

2. Learn to Laugh

As you anticipate each stage your child will go through, it will help to have a sense of humor. My friend Brenda and I were recently laughing at the different stages we've watched our kids go through. And we've found that all parents experience the same ones. There's the "questions" stage, when kids want to know where everything came from and how everything works and we are not able to answer some of their questions. Then there's the "Why?" stage, when kids act defiant and we try to get out of certain situations by saying, "Because I said so." Then there's the "embarrassing" stage, when all we have to do is show up and breathe, and it's embarrassing to our children.

Then there's the "I'm the perfect driver" stage, when they first get their driver's license and are correcting every move we make behind the wheel (because they are freshly acquainted with the driving rules that we've gotten a bit rusty on). Then the "know-it-all" stage happens after they have a high school diploma in their hands (as if that's a huge achievement), and they get especially annoying by their third or fourth year of college (and beyond), when they believe they have special insights into the human psyche (from their psychology 101 class) and believe they singlehandedly could solve the world's problems if they were given the job.

Brenda suggested, "Keep your kids involved in things, especially during the high school know-it-all stage so when they get home they want to eat, do homework, and sleep. Then they won't have as much time to think up how to have an attitude or get into trouble."

3. Learn to Count It Out

One mom told me she "counts to ten" in every situation where she's tempted to blow. Being patient by taking a deep breath and counting to ten makes sure we are not as impulsive and emotional in our responses as our children are in their actions.

4. Learn from Moms Who Have Been There

God frequently speaks to us through the wisdom of others. My friend Judy says, "In addition to praying Scripture over my children, I'm a big believer in talking to godly people who are facing the same things with their kids, or those who made it through difficult situations and can offer sound biblical insight." Again, if you don't have a group of moms who can give you that kind of input, review the suggestions at the end of chapter 1 and find a community of mentor moms.

5. Lean on God's Word

The Bible gives us encouraging words about how to withstand the unexpected or the fearful situations in life. And these same words can apply during seasons of our children's lives when it starts to look like they've taken a turn for the worst.

For example, Psalm 55:22 instructs, "Cast your cares on the LORD and he will sustain you; he will never let the righteous be shaken." And in Psalm 46:1 we are told:

> God is our refuge and strength; an ever-present help
> in trouble. Therefore we will not fear, though the earth

give way and the mountains fall into the heart of the
sea, though its waters roar and foam and the mountains
quake with their surging.

That is a verse that you can apply when you are worried or fearful
about a phase taking place in your child's life. Sometimes it might
seem to you like the earth is giving way and the mountains are falling into the sea when your child is going through a challenging season or dealing with some physical, emotional, or social difficulties.
And yet, according to that passage, God is your ever-present help
in times of trouble.

Scripture also gives us peace as we pray it over our children during difficult or confusing seasons. Judy, whose concerns you read
about at the beginning of this chapter, said, "I wasted a lot of valuable time worrying for nothing when instead, I could have been
praying Scripture verses over my children."

Finding Your Stability

As I mentioned in chapter 1, Scripture says God "does not change
like shifting shadow" (James 1:17). And Psalm 31:2 describes God
as a "rock of refuge" and "strong fortress." I am so grateful that
God is defined in Scripture as our "rock," not our rollercoaster—as
our immovable "house of defence" (KJV) and "stronghold" (NASB),
rather than our up-and-down experience in which we never know
what to expect. And therein lies another secret to keep us from worrying: He is a rock-solid God we can run to in the midst of swirling
changes and uncertainties.

In this world of change—which you and your child are trying to
navigate through—let's look at what *never* changes:

* Our child's appointed lifespan (Psalm 139:16).

* God's comforting presence (Psalm 139:7-12; Hebrews 13:5).

- God's continual compassion and faithfulness (Lamentations 3:22-23).

- God's track record of provision, protection, and loving kindness (Psalm 136).

- The truth and power of God's Word (2 Timothy 3:16).

- God's inseparable love for those who put their trust in Him (Romans 8:38-39).

In addition to never changing, God never misses a thing. Many things can happen in life—even in our own homes—without our knowledge. Our kids can pull a fast one past us. But nothing takes God by surprise. And with Him at your right hand, you are in a place of stability. In Psalm 16:8, David said: "I have set the LORD always before me. Because he is at my right hand, I will not be shaken."

It's Up to You

Do you have that kind of confidence? Are you able to say, "I will not be shaken"? You can. With the Lord as your Right-Hand Man, you can stand firmly and be a steady, immovable force in your child's life no matter what he or she is going through.

It's up to you. Will you wring your hands with worry during the difficult seasons your child goes through? Or will you trust that God has walked through it before you and can help you navigate it as well? In the days ahead, I pray you will see your *season of worry* as a *time to trust* so that God can usher you into an exciting new *phase of peace*.

Putting It into Practice
....

Praying to the Immovable One

Lord God, You are my Rock of Strength and my Stronghold. I am so glad Scripture does not define You as my Driftwood, never in the same place twice. Or my Stream that is Constantly Running. Or my Temperamental Power, in which I never know what to expect. Instead, Scripture says you are my Rock, my Refuge, my Strong Tower. Immovable. Unchanging. Steady. Always in the same place. I don't need to run after you and try to catch You. I don't need to try to find You because You've never left. And I don't need to constantly be on guard for fear that You might shift or change. You are my Rock, not my Roller Coaster—my *immovable Rock of Refuge to whom I can always go.*[17]

Thank You, God, that in spite of my child's different stages of development and growth, You are the same, reliable God in season and out. Help me to be a mom who responds, rather than reacts, and who learns to laugh and patiently encourage my child. Help me to lean on Your unchanging Word through whatever lies ahead.

I depend on You as my Strong Tower (Psalm 46:1), my Fortress and my Deliverer (Psalm 18:2) and my Righteous Right Hand (Psalm 16:8). And thank You that You can get my children through *every* season of their lives.

Becoming a Worry-Free Mom
—in Community

For Thought or Discussion: Which stage of life is your child in right now? If there isn't a word for it, come up with a creative title of your own and share it with the group. (Make note of the other moms whose children are in the same or similar stages.)

1. What are you learning about God and your child in this stage of his/her life?

2. Read the following verses and write all the ways God is a help to you in your times of uncertainty or trouble:

   Psalm 62:5-7—

   Psalm 71:3—

   Psalm 91:1-2—

   Isaiah 26:4—

3. Consider your child's current phase or stage and list some practical ways that you can:

   Respond, not react—

   Keep a sense of humor—

   Express patience—

   Learn from other moms—

Lean on God's Word—

4. Was there a specific verse in this chapter that stood out
   to you? Write it in the space below, and let it help you
   through this current season of your child's life and the
   seasons ahead. (You may want to insert your child's
   name into that verse as well.)

5

You're Hanging Out with Who?

∙∙∙

Secret 5: Giving Their Social Life to God

Terri battled fear, worry, and stress for nearly 30 years as she raised her two children into adulthood. For her, one of the most fearful aspects of parenting was watching her children make friendships and enter social situations that didn't appear to be healthy.

"My kids went to public schools in a pretty rough district," Terri said. "I remember my daughter having middle school classes with a lot of students in the 'Goth' group. I had prayed that she would be wise about the friendships she made and not negatively influenced by others.

"One day she came home from school and we were talking about her classmates and if there was anything I could pray about for her. She said 'Mom, you know the Goth kids look real scary. But deep down inside they are just like me—a regular person.'

"I realized then that my daughter saw them through the eyes of Jesus. I was the one worried about the Goth influence and God was directing my daughter to remind me of how God saw and cared for those kids too."

While Terri's daughter remained unscathed by her friendships with the Goth crowd, her son brought more fears into her life as he went off to college and joined a fraternity against his parents' wishes.

"We found out the guys in the fraternity who were twenty-one were allowed to drink alcohol in the fraternity house, and so were the alumni," Terri said. She was concerned that her son, Kevin, who was still underage, would face pressure to drink.

"Kevin assured us that he would make the right choices and that we needed to trust him. I was in prayer constantly. I imagined that the peer pressure for him to join in was intense."

But as was the case with her daughter and the Goth crowd, Kevin was not negatively influenced by the fraternity house, as Terri feared. In fact, just the opposite happened.

"After a couple of years in the fraternity house, my son decided to run for president of the house and make it a nondrinking, alcohol-free place. He won the election, and many of the seniors moved out as a result because the decision to change was not popular, even with the alumni. I praised God for giving Kevin the conviction, strength, and obedience to take a stand against drinking. What began as a fearful course of events to me—his joining the fraternity and the exposure to so much ungodly behavior—resulted in praise and a testimony of obedience by my son not giving in to the ways of the world."

Terri said that during the years she was raising her children, she had prayed Proverbs 1:10 for them: "My son, if sinful men entice you, do not give in to them."

Terri had worried that both her daughter and son would be negatively influenced by the kids they were around. But in both cases, her children ended up positively influencing the kids around them.

The day will come, if it hasn't already, that you will not like or approve of the other children, teenagers, or young adults your child wants to be around. We can control that for only so long, and then our children will eventually choose their own friends. That is when we need to pray for God to search our hearts and give us wisdom. Are we afraid of what we don't know? Are we assuming our children will be followers rather than leaders? Are we underestimating God's ability to use our children to influence others?

Why We Care So Much

When you and I were little, it meant the world to us to be accepted by other girls our age and truly liked for who we were. Yes, it would've been great to be popular and liked by everyone. But just knowing we had friends—or even one best friend—was what really mattered.

I don't know that we ever outgrow that until we discover how accepted we are by God, who sent His son, Jesus, to die on the cross for us and redeem us of our sin. Once we realize our great significance to God, being accepted by others loses its hold and importance in our lives. But until we reach that point, it remains important to us to be accepted and truly liked for who we are.

No wonder we worry so much about our children's friends or lack of them.

Krissy's Concerns

Krissy is an elementary school teacher and mom of a nine-year-old daughter and six-year-old son who attend her school. Even with her presence there on the campus, she worries about her children's social development and their ability to have friends.

"Most of my concerns for them now are related to their social life," Krissy told me. "They both tell me they don't have any friends. They choose to spend their recess and lunch in my classroom because they aren't making connections with their peers. I find myself constantly worried about whether or not they are being accepted by others. I worry if they are fitting in and making friends. I worry that they are viewed as weird or different. They get emotional easily, and I wonder if they are being made fun of.

"As an elementary school teacher, I have seen how cruel kids can be to each other. I've seen how they treat each other when they think adults aren't looking. I fear that my children will become subject to the harshness of the world around them before they are ready to deal with it in an appropriate way. I find myself being anxious about the door opening and one of them being in tears because someone didn't accept them for who they are."

Krissy's daughter was recently diagnosed with ADHD by a doctor and a child psychiatrist. "She will get emotional and her reactions to situations are often not age-appropriate," Krissy said. "She's been on numerous medications, and each time one doesn't work it becomes more distressing. She gets frustrated with her own actions at times. She often gets depressed because she has to bring home an insane amount of homework because she couldn't focus in the classroom.

"I see her struggle every day. Sometimes I watch her from a distance. She sits on the sidelines and rarely interacts with others around her. She fidgets, looks at the ceiling, or plays with random things like her fingers. If she does interact with others, it is often in an inappropriate or immature way. She gets overly excitable to the point that she appears out of control. I am afraid that as she gets older that the other kids will start to notice that her behaviors are not 'normal' and that she will be rejected."

Krissy's son has had social difficulties as well. He's in first grade, and she sees a lot of the same characteristics in him that her daughter exhibited at that age.

"I am afraid he is going to struggle in the same way she has."

Krissy's worries and frustrations are not unique. Like any mom, she wants to protect her children, fix the problems, help them adjust, make them "normal."

"I wish I could shield them both from the frustrations that are ahead," she said. "I'm the mommy. A mommy is supposed to make everything better. She's supposed to kiss the hurts and fix everything. I can't fix this. I can't put a Band-Aid on it and make it go away.

"I have to admit that I have not found complete peace in this situation. God is still dealing with me on a daily basis. It's hard to watch your child struggle. I am learning to accept that God has created my children in His image. He has a plan and a purpose for each of the trials that we go through, even as children. I am learning to trust that He will use these situations for good."

Krissy is beginning to do that by changing her focus: "One thing I have learned is that all too often we dwell on whether or not we are accepted by those around us. What we *should* focus on instead is the fact God accepts us just as we are, with all of our quirks and imperfections. He values us so much that He took the time to create us individually in His likeness. He loves us so much that He sent His Son to die for our sins so that we may spend eternity with Him.

"So rather than worry about how my children are viewed or accepted by the world, I'm going to focus on their value in the Lord and teach them to do the same. Rather than worry about teaching them to deal with the rejection of the world, I'm going to steer their hearts and minds towards the love and acceptance of their Creator, who thinks they are pretty awesome just the way they are."

Our Need for Acceptance

Mom, do you worry about your own acceptance? Do you have trouble making friends? Do you place an unhealthy importance on friendships or overemphasize how important it is to be liked? Sometimes our children pick up their ideas and values concerning friendships, relationships, and marriage from what they see in us.

I think it's natural for us, as humans, to struggle with whether or not we are accepted. No matter what age we are, within our humanity, we are crying out to be loved, accepted, cared for, and (more specifically to women) cherished. So I think, as moms, we automatically project those concerns onto our children as well. Will they be liked by other children? Will they be loved and accepted for who they really are? Will someone want to marry them someday? And when we think or see that they're feeling unaccepted, we take it personally, as if that wound is our very own.

Rather than worry that our children won't be accepted by others, we can, like Krissy, show them how accepted they are by us and God. In doing that, we help them to not become people pleasers, hoping for acceptance everywhere they go. Rather, we help mold them into God pleasers.

God's View of Us

In God's Word, we are told that if we are "in Christ"—meaning if we are trusting in Him alone for our salvation—we are:

- God's child (John 1:12)
- Christ's friend (John 15:15)
- a saint (Ephesians 1:1)
- bought with a price, and therefore belong to God (1 Corinthians 6:19-20)
- adopted as God's child (Ephesians 1:5)
- redeemed and forgiven (Colossians 1:14)
- complete in Christ (Colossians 2:10)
- fearfully and wonderfully made (Psalm 139:14)
- more valuable to God than the sparrows (Matthew 10:31)
- inseparable from God's love (Romans 8:38-39)
- God's "masterpiece" (Ephesians 2:10 NLT)
- God's "temple" (1 Corinthians 3:16)

- God's co-worker (2 Corinthians 6:1)

- a citizen of heaven (Philippians 3:20)

Now consider those descriptions above in light of your children. Your children's quirks when they're younger and dysfunctions when they're older don't go unnoticed by God, who knows every detail about them.

A Forever Friend

I remember my first day of kindergarten. I felt awkward because I didn't know anyone in my classroom and I feared not having friends. I remember praying to Jesus that I would have a special friend—or several. I had learned from the time I was little that Jesus is always there and I could call on Him in prayer.

Throughout elementary and middle school, friends were extremely important to me. Perhaps more than they should have been, as I remember a lot of "girl drama" and being distraught at what others thought of me or if someone wouldn't talk to me or if someone was somebody *else's* best friend and not mine.

When I entered high school I was quite social, but still very much into friends rather than boyfriends. Then I began a dating relationship the night I graduated from high school, and it lasted four years—four unhealthy, often very lonely years. Those were the years I grew in my relationship with Christ because I was constantly needing companionship and longing to feel accepted and loved for who I was.

During my third year of college, when I was feeling the stress of this dating relationship, I penned (literally) a poem that described the hollows of my heart and where I learned to turn on those days when I was feeling alone. In the midst of thinking I might never be wanted or loved by a man, I wrote this:

Lord, when I'm lonely and want to talk,
Let me bring my thoughts to you.
When I'm discouraged 'cause no one's around
Remind me that You're always there.
When I look to someone for encouragement
Remind me that You are my source of strength.
When I want to be with someone who cares,
Remind me that You are my closest friend.
When I expect others to meet my needs
Remind me only You can satisfy.
When I feel I need some comfort and love
Gently remind me of my Father above.

Looking back at the time that poem was written, I can see how the yearning of my heart was to have someone know me. And God had assured me through His Word that I was known. I wanted to have someone love me. And through His Word, He graciously made known to me I was loved. I wanted to be filled, and He assured me that only He can satisfy.[18] Knowing that Jesus is my forever friend has helped me not to worry about my daughter making friends. It is my prayer that He will comfort her with His presence during times when she feels lonely too.

When God Softens Hearts

There may be times when your child comes home from school and tells you about someone who is making their life miserable. As a mom, I know you want to go scratch that person's eyes out. But let me tell you a story of how my mom reacted to a situation like that and how it helped me learn something that I still rely on today.

When I was in sixth grade, a seventh-grade girl who was part of the popular crowd repeatedly made mean remarks to me. She would look at me and say things like "I hate you" and "You're ugly." She wasn't someone I wanted to be friends with. In fact, she was just an older girl picking on me. But it made me feel awful. I remember telling my mom about this girl and how she made me feel. My mom said, "Just smile sweetly at her, and pretty soon she won't be able to think of any reason to be mean to you."

I didn't want to smile sweetly at her. I didn't want to have *any* type of exchange with her. I just wanted this girl to move out of town so I never had to be around her again.

One day, as I contemplated how I could convince my parents into letting me go to a different school so I could avoid this girl, my mom came into my room and prayed with me that God would "soften the heart" of the person who was being hateful toward me.

The next morning, I repeated that prayer on my way to school. "God, please soften her heart toward me so she's not so mean."

Before school started, that girl walked by me and didn't say a word. Either she didn't notice me, or she just didn't have time to be mean. I was relieved. The next day, the same thing happened. She ignored me. *Yes! Maybe the harassment was finally over.* The day after that, a friend of hers called me out for having pants that were too short, and this girl who was usually so hateful said to her friend, "Leave her alone. It's not her fault." She then looked at me as if to say, "I'm sorry."

Could Miss Hateful have gone from hating me to *defending* me?

I don't recall her ever being mean to me again after that. From that I learned that God can not only help me be more confident as I walk into situations that I dread, but He can change hearts. And He can change the hearts of the children who are bullying yours, of the teenage girls whom your daughter is trying to befriend, of the players on the team who want nothing to do with your son, or the people in your children's lives who seem to have it out for them.

Had my mom chosen to talk to the school principal about the girl who was bullying me, it probably would've made my situation worse with that girl. And if my mom had just wrung her hands and told me how worried she was about me, it might have given me an ulcer! But because she taught me to pray for a softened heart, I learned some valuable lessons for life and a secret that helps me not worry when it comes to how others treat me or my child:

- instead of worrying, take your situation to God

- pray for God to soften hearts, and your perspective (dislike) of that person will change

- God is concerned about the same things you are concerned about, but He can actually *do* something about them

- God is in the business of coming through for those who lean on Him to meet their needs

Ever since, I have often prayed that God would soften the heart of someone who was causing me grief—a friend or boyfriend who wasn't speaking to me, a family member, a college professor, my boss at my first few jobs, coworkers while working for a newspaper, women I've worked with (and disagreed with) in ministry. And every time I have asked God to specifically soften someone's heart toward me, He has.

I believe you know where I'm heading with this. When moms rush in to rescue—or when they choose to worry—they are teaching their kids to rely on mom or themselves, not God and His ability to change the situation by softening a heart.

There are examples in Scripture of God changing the hearts of people, especially hardened, stubborn, unwilling-to-change people.[19] And God can still change hearts today—the heart of your child's teacher, the hearts of other children who don't like your child, the hearts of young men or women who shouldn't be dating your child, the hearts of parents who have misunderstood situations, the hearts of your children's bosses at work, and the list goes on.

Can you find opportunities to pray with your children that God will soften or change the heart of someone who is causing them grief in their life? If not, you go ahead and start praying for the softening. I believe God will hear and act.

Intercession or Interference?

Brenda Jean, who has one child, a 21-year-old daughter, shared with me that her heart has been grieved over the fact that her daughter got engaged to a young man that both Brenda and her daughter didn't believe was God's best for her.

"God made it clear to her [prior to the engagement] that this young man was not the one for her, but she has so much 'invested' in this relationship," Brenda said. "Adding to this scenario are several other confirmations from the Holy Spirit over the last year and a half about who her future spouse would be (some very specific details that reveal it is not this young man) and she shares with me about every two months that she still thinks often about these promises and expresses her uncertainty of the future of this relationship."

Brenda believes her daughter knows God is asking her to end this relationship, but shame and embarrassment keep her from doing so. "Her fear is wrapped up in the idea that no one will love her, and it reveals to me that she has forgotten her 'First Love' [Christ]."

Like any mom would, Brenda wants to help her daughter break free from this relationship that her daughter doesn't feel strong enough to end. Yet, God recently made it clear to Brenda that she needs to let *Him* do the work.

"One of the things God has been pressing me on during this time is to trust Him, believe His Word when He says something, and wait for His work to be completed (without my help!). I often find myself wanting to know how God is working, asking Him to include me in on His plans for her, or to give me a visible sign. Well, this really isn't trust, is it?"

Brenda said having a dedicated quiet time with God in the morning has helped her rely on God and the way *He* wants to do things, instead of taking the situation back into her hands and trying to work it out herself.

"I have also been steadfast in prayer for my daughter and have opened up and shared with some sisters who hold me accountable and pray for both of us at the same time. This prayer and accountability has really sustained me through some of the tougher moments."

Recently, though, Brenda said God made it very clear to her that her attempts at intercession for her daughter were actually interference.

"During personal prayer just about three weeks ago, God specifically told me I was to stop spoon-feeding my daughter with the daily Scripture encouragements and 'leading' conversations to encourage her to remember His promises," Brenda said. "He showed me that this was sustaining her in the compromised life she's leading, and that she couldn't get hungry enough for Him to go looking for Him on her own. In essence, I was interfering with His work. It was difficult for me to understand how leaving Scripture notes or prayers on her vanity, or sending her an encouraging text could be interfering, but I've walked long enough with the Lord to know when He commands something, I'd better do it! So I did..."

Once Brenda backed off, God really got to work, she said.

"The change in my daughter was almost immediate—I'd say within a week. This is when she had her own revelation about how compromised her walk had become. I am humbled and absolutely in awe at how quickly God worked when I got out of the way. It's as if He swooped in the moment I stepped back! Since that time, her hostility toward me has disappeared, she has returned to being the kind, compassionate and others-focused person she's been prior to these last few years."

Brenda told me recently that her daughter finally called off the engagement, but continues to see the young man off and on, in her continued difficulty to entirely let the relationship go. And yet, Brenda is keeping her eyes on God and His promises, instead of worrying.

"My daughter is learning to trust God's timing, to ask for His guidance, and to stay close to Him. And I have learned (though not perfectly yet!), to be silent unless asked for advice. We spent several months barely speaking, as she pulled further and further away from me. If it were not for faithful friends and prayer warriors and God's Word, I wouldn't have made it through this time very successfully at all."

Brenda and I aren't suggesting that "backing off" is a rule for every mom. Your notes, words of encouragement, and intercessory prayers for your child may be exactly what God wants you to do. But in this mom's case, she firmly believed God was saying "Move aside and let Me work." It's difficult to do. But once we realize God can parent our children better than we can, there is an incredible peace that overtakes us. And in this mom's case, God *did* work, once she backed off.

Showing Them God's Love

What can you and I learn from an unhealthy or a spiritually mismatched dating relationship? How can you and I grow through a situation in which our child chooses to be around someone we personally don't approve of?

Chances are, the person your son or daughter has chosen to be around (and whom you don't approve of) has his or her own set of wounds that has *caused* him or her to be the kind of person you don't want your child around.

How was that person raised? you might have thought at one point or another. Well, that's a good question. Because it's possible he wasn't raised by a dad who showed him how to treat a young woman. It's possible she wasn't raised by a dad or mom who showed her she was significant and she didn't have to dress a certain way to get attention. It's possible his rambunctiousness or his or her rebellion is out of pain that you know nothing about.

Their Unhealthy Influences

We can pray that our children will be leaders and positively influence everyone they associate with. But in reality, there will come times when your child *is* being negatively influenced by another. Whether it's a dating relationship that has you worried or a rough group of friends your child is hanging out with, God can handle that situation too. And He can teach us a lot about ourselves—and His love for others—in the process.

This is how you can experience peace if your child is friends with, dating, going into business with, or planning to marry someone you don't approve of:

Pray for That Person You Don't Approve Of

Our first instinct is to pray for our own child's protection. But have you considered it's very possible no one is praying for the child or young adult you want to protect your child from? God may very well have teamed that person up with *your* child because someone in *your* household would begin praying for him or her. As you begin to pray for that person, God will change your heart toward him or her. I guarantee it. This is always my first line of advice when moms come to me, in a panic, that their daughters or sons are beginning to date unbelievers. You can fight it with your child, and very possibly damage your relationship with that child. Or you can fight it in the heavenly realm through prayer, making yourself available to God in any way that He wants to work in the situation.

Picture Their Hurts

Inappropriate behavior on the part of other children—young or older—often comes from wounds, inappropriate parenting, or neglect. Consider that this person who is a negative or unhealthy influence on your child has been exposed to something negative or unhealthy too. As you begin to ponder their heart and picture their hurt, God will give you a compassion for them and possibly show you how to pray for them further.

Pray Scripture over Your Child

As you pray Scripture verses for your child, you are praying not according to your wisdom or your desires, but God's. If you're like me, you can sometimes slip into the mode of trying to instruct God on how to best handle the situation. But God doesn't need our suggestions. In fact, our measly suggestions to the all-knowing, all-capable God are an insult to Him. He knows far better than us how to work all things for good in our children's lives. As we pray God's Word over our children, we are praying His will and His wisdom over them.

My friend Judy learned this while her son was growing up and experienced such peace in doing so.

"I recently began praying Scripture over my kids, plugging their names in the verses to make my requests more specific," Judy said. Some of her favorite prayers are...

- "Create in [Jason] a clean heart, O God, and renew a right spirit within [him]" (Psalm 51:10).

- "May [Steve] listen to the way of wisdom and be led in the paths of uprightness" (see Proverbs 4:11).

- "Give [Sherry] a great desire to accept Your word, God, and store up Your commands within [her] so [her] ears will turn to Your wisdom" (see Proverbs 2:1-2).

Judy said, "Just speaking people's names into the verses makes the prayer requests more real and meaningful to me."

At the end of this chapter, you'll have an opportunity to pray Scripture for your own children so you can experience that peace too.

God's Work in *You*

As you pray for those who are near to your children, ponder their hearts and persevere in God's love for them. God may transform you from a mom who worries about negative influences on your children to a mom who prays for those who are near to your children. I know it would be easier if God just pulled certain individuals out of your children's sphere of influence and you could pray for people whom you'd *like* to pray for. But God often doesn't work that way. He works on us, refining and smoothing those rough corners of our hearts so we truly know what Calvary love looks like. Jesus prayed, while on the cross, for those who were mocking Him, spitting at Him, and cursing His name. With that in mind, the least we can do for that One who died for us is pray for those whose hearts He still wants to reach.

As you pray for God to soften the hearts of those around your children, you may even find that the heart He softens the most is *yours*.

Putting It into Practice
· ·
Praying for Your Child's Relationships

Let's pray Scripture over your child and his or her relationships by inserting your child's name in the blanks:

> Lord God, thank You that you have searched_____ _____ and you know _____. You discern _____'s coming out and _____'s lying down; you are familiar with all _____'s ways (Psalm 139:1,3). Help _____ choose friends carefully (Proverbs 12:26). If sinful men (or women) entice _____, help her to not give in to them (Proverbs 1:10). May the perverse of heart be far from _____; may (he/she) have nothing to do with what is evil (Psalm 101:4). Finally, help _____, like Jesus, to grow in wisdom and stature, and in favor with God and man (Luke 2:52).

· ·
Becoming a Worry-Free Mom
—in Community
· ·

For Thought or Discussion: What did you learn as a child that you can pass on to your own child about healthy or unhealthy friendships?

1. Is there someone near your child whom you don't approve of? Maybe you are hoping your child will find a friend/boyfriend/girlfriend at this point. Write out your concern here, as a prayer to God, realizing He already has

it all in His control. (Sometimes writing out a concern is a way of releasing that worry and finally letting it go.)

2. Look up the following verses and write down what each has to say concerning friendships or close associations:

Psalm 1:1—

Proverbs 1:10—

Proverbs 12:26—

Proverbs 16:28—

Proverbs 17:9—

Proverbs 17:17—

Proverbs 18:24—

Proverbs 22:11—

Proverbs 22:24—

Proverbs 27:6—

Proverbs 27:9-10—

3. Circle or highlight any verses above that would be helpful to share with your child.

4. Write out one or two of the above verses in the space below with your child's name inserted into the verse(s), and use as a guide for praying for your child's social life.

6

I Wish That Had Never Happened

Secret 6: Trusting God's Faultless Filter

How will this affect my children?

I know you've asked that question as the unexpected came your way.

Kathleen asked it too as she learned her husband was leaving her and their four children ranging in age from 13-22.

"My husband, who was such a great father to our four kids, has left, filed for divorce, and is now trapped in the sins of divorce, adultery, and alcoholism, like his own dad. Because I was a stay-at-home mom for all those years, I have had to get a full-time job. I know all of this hasn't caught God off guard, but it certainly has thrown me and the kids."

Connie worries about how her children will be affected not by divorce, but by being around family members who do not share her and her husband's worldview.

"I worry about my children's protection," Connie said. "Many members of my family are unbelievers who don't share the same beliefs and values that my husband and I do...So we are not comfortable with our children being around them for an extended period of time, if at all. We want to protect our kids from things that are not age-appropriate, including certain language and topics of conversation, and unhealthy environments. We want to instill biblical principles into them, which is a challenge when they're in an environment that is the opposite of how things are at home."

Angela says, "When my daughter was five years old, she spent the night at a friend's house and they watched the movie *Titanic*. I *never* would have let her watch that movie at her age. I realized then that my view of what I thought was appropriate for my child at the time was not necessarily the same as everyone else's. Even though I felt I knew this family, in hindsight, I didn't. It was a learning experience as a parent, as well as for my child."

I'm sure you know by now that there is no perfect environment in which to raise a child. We live in a fallen world of death, drugs, divorce, violence in video games and down the street, inappropriate scenes and language on television, immorality next door, pornography on the Internet, and explicit lyrics blasting from stereos in cars that pull up next to ours. It is *impossible* to shield our children from every negative influence that exists in this world. All we can hope for is to raise them according to the principles in God's Word so that when they come upon compromising situations, they will have the discernment (and a clear voice from the Holy Spirit) that equips them to know right from wrong.

However, when you're doing all you can and your child still experiences something you regret, remember this: God can *filter out the garbage* and *fill in the gaps* when it comes to your children's bad or missed experiences.

Our Childhood Baggage

In chapter 2, I addressed our fear of the unknown—the "what ifs" that plague us almost daily—when it comes to our children. Add to that our own baggage, and I believe every mom can think of a situation in her past that she wouldn't want to be repeated with her own children.

Going back to Connie, who expressed concerns about the unhealthy environment her children are in when they are around her family: her greatest fear is that her two young daughters, ages two and four, will not be safe from the predators in this world.

"One of my biggest fears, when Emma was born, was that she would be inappropriately touched or molested by a 'trusted' male in the family. A key reason for my fear is that's what happened to me when I was in grade school. It happened in my aunt's home, with a cousin. I spent a lot of time at that house and often stayed the night because there was only one of me and I had five cousins, and it was much more fun to be at their home where all the other kids were."

Connie was in what she (and her family) assumed was a safe environment when she faced that harmful and threatening situation. She fears not being able to determine what is completely safe for her daughters as well.

You and I can either (1) worry and possibly repeat the cycle of our pain and dysfunction with our own children, or (2) choose to do things differently and stop the cycle of unhealthy behavior. I want to be a mom who stops—instead of repeats—the cycle of dysfunction I dealt with in my upbringing. So does Connie. And I've talked to many other moms, as well, who are set on doing the same.

Marilyn, a survivor of child abuse, is determined to do all she can to make a safe environment for her daughters, who are nine and eleven years old.

While it's difficult for Marilyn to understand the *why* behind crimes against a child, she knows God is growing her trust in Him as she places her own daughters in His loving hands.

"I used to fret about my dysfunctional issues influencing my daughters, but I've accepted we are all under God's grace and we all have our own hurtful issues and sin to deal with. Sometimes we unintentionally pass on to our children the things our parents taught us, like anger, impatience, and fear, but God is bigger.

"I struggle with fear. One big moment for me occurred during a counseling session when I realized that bad things could and might happen to my children, but they would survive. I'm a survivor of childhood abuse at the hands of my parents and others, and it has made me who I am. My children see me continue to cling to Jesus and try to overcome what the abuse has done to me, and that's okay.

"I struggle a lot with fear because of all that happened to me when no one was there to rescue me. I remind myself that fear is from the enemy, and I go to Scripture. I also set boundaries—like no sleepovers. Books and articles I've read encourage this. It keeps my mind at ease, and the kids don't feel like there are exceptions.

"I do wonder if I've ever put them in a compromised position, and I may have without knowing it. But God is big enough, and I give them to Him. This is not heaven. There is a lot of sin in this world and, statistically speaking, things could happen. That's been hard for me to accept, but I'm ready for it and I'll do my part to protect them."

As Marilyn stated, how we deal with our own past hurts can help our children learn how to deal with them too. Marilyn's children are seeing her cling to Jesus. What are your children seeing?

Our Children's Baggage

In some cases, our baggage isn't the only factor affecting our children. Some of our kids come with baggage of their own.

Dawn G. and her husband adopted a seven-year-old girl a few years ago. This girl had a history that Dawn wished hadn't happened. Yet she relies daily on God to help her and her husband undo the damage and give this child a new future and hope.

"Our primary concerns at this stage in her life are helping her work through her grief journey as well as the issues she faces from past trauma and neglect. We work with her therapist and school to help with behavioral challenges."

Dawn says it hasn't been easy. There are days she wonders if she's in over her head.

"I have a tendency to get caught up in the stress of the moment, especially when our daughter is having a difficult day. Worries, stress, and fear come all too easily. That is why I must continually remind myself that God is in control and that He connected our lives with that of our beautiful child. When challenges threaten to weigh us down, we go to the Lord in prayer and beg for His peace, mercy, and a measurable dose of patience!

"Older adopted children enter their new families with established personalities, memories, and incredible grief. Part of this pain is often released through extreme behaviors and boundary testing. They want to know if their new parents are consistent and if they are truly in a safe place. Parenting the hurting child requires stamina, resolve, patience, and most of all, love. I find it hard to let go and trust God when we are in the midst of a particularly difficult day. My goal, and my prayer, is to be able to hear God's still small voice even in the toughest trial."

If our responsibility as mom, stepmom, foster mom, or adopted mom was to right all the wrongs that have happened or continue to happen in our children's lives, it would be a daunting—if not impossible—task. We would all fail miserably. But here's the secret: God doesn't expect us to filter out our child's bad experiences or fill in the gaps with what more they need. That is *His* job. He asks us to simply trust His track record.

God's Track Record

In the Bible, we read accounts of God's impressive track record of filtering out (or filling in the gaps) for some unfortunate Hebrew children who lived thousands of years ago—children who grew up to be great leaders and heroes of the Bible.

Molded by Pain

There is an amazing story in the Bible about a man who should've been scarred for life after all he experienced as a teenager and young adult. Yet his is one of the most inspiring stories in the Bible—a story that affirms the sovereignty of God and His ability to turn what the world meant for evil into good.

Joseph was the favored son of Jacob, and his ten older brothers knew it and hated him for it. Joseph had already lost his mother, who died while giving birth to his younger brother. When he told his older brothers about a dream in which God had made him ruler over the entire family, and the entire land as well, his brothers plotted to kill him. After throwing him in a dark pit where he was alone and helpless, they decided to sell him as a slave to some travelling Midianites. Upon returning home, they told their father Joseph had been killed by a wild animal.

So at the formative age of just 17 years old, Joseph was abandoned by his brothers, thought to be dead by his father, and sold to Midianite traders, who then took him to Egypt and sold him to one of Pharaoh's officials.

Joseph, who could have understandably been bitter and depressed about his circumstance, made the best of it. He set his mind to being the best servant in the house of the official, and was soon promoted and trusted with the official's entire household. But when the official's wife tried to seduce him, Joseph ran from her (good for him!). She then falsely accused him of attempted rape.

Joseph was arrested and thrown into prison...even though he had done the right thing and avoided that woman's advances. Again, he refused to let his plight get him down. He did his best in prison as well, and was soon promoted by the warden and placed in charge of all the other prisoners. And despite a promise that he would be remembered—and possibly released—for correctly interpreting a dream of one of the prisoners who was restored to office, Joseph stayed there in prison *another two years*, having been forgotten.

Yet God didn't forget about Joseph. Later he was given an opportunity to help interpret the Pharaoh's dreams (with God's help, of course). As a result he was promoted to Pharaoh's right hand and became second in charge of all of Egypt! This man Joseph, who should have had baggage and bitterness unlike anything we've seen, was still a humble, forgiving, God-fearing man whom God continued to bless.

Any mom would be horrified at what Joseph went through from the time he was a teenager. Yet God filtered through everything he endured to build his character and shape him into a man who could rule a nation. Would you, as a mom, have been able to guess that *one bad thing after another* was actually preparing your son for the greatest blessing he and his family would ever know? That's exactly what happened as Joseph ended up saving his jealous-turned-repentant brothers and his loving father years later during a severe famine that swept over Egypt and the surrounding countries. Because of Joseph's position in Egypt, the twelve tribes of Israel were spared starvation during the famine.[20]

Unaffected by the Darkness

In chapter 1, I told you a little about Moses—his insecurities and weaknesses and how God chose to use him anyway because he was a man who would depend on God. Let's take a moment now to review his upbringing, for he too should have been scarred for life.

Moses was three months old when he was set out on the Nile

River in a floating bassinet made of papyrus and pitch so he wouldn't be found in his home and slaughtered, as was the fate of any Hebrew baby boy in Egypt. When Pharaoh's daughter discovered him while bathing in the Nile, she had compassion on him. Moses' sister was nearby to suggest a Hebrew nurse for the baby, which, by God's providence, turned out to be Moses' own mother, whom Pharoah's daughter even paid to nurse Moses until he was weaned. Scripture says, "When the child grew older, [Moses' mother] took him to Pharaoh's daughter and he became her son" (Exodus 2:10).

Can you picture this? At three or four years old, this child started living like Egyptian royalty. And he was exposed to the sorcery, the godlessness, the dark oppressive practices of the Egyptians. There would have been no further godly instruction for him once he set foot in that palace. One would think he would've been irreparably corrupted. Or that he would have at least forgotten where he came from, and to whom was his allegiance.

And yet God's hand of protection—and His faultless filter—was on Moses' life.

Scripture tells us that "after Moses had grown up, he went out to where *his own people* were and watched them at their hard labor. He saw an Egyptian beating a Hebrew, *one of his own people*. Glancing this way and that and seeing no one, he killed the Egyptian and hid him in the sand."[21]

You would think Moses would have identified himself with the Egyptians by then, not the Hebrews. Yet he murdered the Egyptian because of how he saw him treating "his own people." Perhaps the quick, efficient murder is one of the things he learned while growing up Egyptian. But, Moses didn't get much thanks for this act of mercy toward his own people. Scripture tells us:

> The next day [Moses] went out and saw two Hebrews fighting. He asked the one in the wrong, "Why are you

hitting your fellow Hebrew?" The man said, "Who made you ruler and judge over us? Are you thinking of killing me as you killed the Egyptian?" Then Moses was afraid and thought, "What I did must have become known." When Pharaoh heard of this, he tried to kill Moses, but Moses fled from Pharaoh and went to live in Midian (Exodus 2:13-15).

Talk about a bad couple of days! After defending one of his own people, Moses was alienated by both the Hebrews and the Egyptians. Without any people to turn to, he fled to the Midianites (remember those guys who bought young Joseph and sold him to the Egyptians?). While living among them he eventually found a wife and started a family, and stayed away from everyone else for 40 years.

By the time Moses had surely forgotten all about his life in Egypt, God sent him back to Pharaoh to ask for the release of the Hebrew slaves. Talk about having to face your old wounds! God used this man Moses, who should have had some serious baggage against both the Egyptians and the Hebrews, to be the one to free His people.

God obviously had a filter on Moses' life too. He let in what needed to go in (Moses' memories that he was a Hebrew), and kept out what He didn't want to damage him (the negative influences of the godless Egyptians).

If you could have done so, would you have tried to stop the negative influences Moses was exposed to during his growing-up years? Any mom would! Yet who would've guessed that God would use those very circumstances to build the character of a man who became one of the Bible's greatest heroes?

The Faithfulness of God

In both Joseph's and Moses' lives, God did a filtering work that kept the bad from harming them and brought about results that had a positive effect on the lives of many others. And I believe God is faithful to do his filtering work in our children today as well. He knows far better than we do what needs to be filtered out so it doesn't affect our kids. And He is able to determine what our children can handle. In that way, God acts as a shield for our children.

Psalm 18:30 says:

> As for God, his way is perfect:
> The LORD's word is flawless;
> he *shields* all who take refuge in him.

Psalm 28:7 tells us,

> The LORD is my strength and my *shield*;
> my heart trusts in him, and he helps me.

Furthermore, Psalm 84:11 says,

> For the LORD God is a sun and *shield*;
> the LORD bestows favor and honor;
> no good thing does he withhold
> from those whose walk is blameless.

God is both a *sun* and *shield*—not only illuminating our path, but protecting us on it as well. God has many ways of shielding us and showing Himself faithful through situations we wish hadn't happened.

Here are some of the ways that God protects us and our children:

He Helps Us Gain Wisdom from Our Experience

Angela, whose daughter saw the movie *Titanic* at the tender age of five, said that situation taught them both something. "I had to trust my instinct for my child even if someone else didn't have the same convictions about a certain activity or movie. That situation opened the door for my daughter and me to have a good talk. She knew, going forward, that if she was ever in doubt that I would let her do something, she needed to say, 'I need to ask my mom.'"

He Helps Us Bring Things to Light

Once Connie began talking about how she had been molested as a child, her family members realized how easily something like that could happen with their own children. They have joined her in setting boundaries and being more cautious.

Connie says, "What brought peace over this situation for me was bringing it to light. I believe Satan was using this to drive a wedge between my husband and me, to paralyze me and bring about division in our family. So far I had only told one person about this, years and years ago. The biggest lie that was playing over and over in my mind was that I couldn't tell my husband about it.

"One day, when Emma was just a few months old, as my husband and I sat down to eat, I broke down in tears and shared with him what had happened. That in itself brought relief and a huge sense of peace, and I knew God was there with us. I proceeded to share these things with my mom (since Emma spends so much time with her), my sisters (who have sons Emma's age, and they spend a lot of time together), and more recently my sister-in-law (who has a son Emma's age and were recently found playing something hidden). Bringing light to the situation was where the Lord met me to bring healing. Now my family sees how easily this could happen, and understands and respects our desire to have these boundaries with the children as they spend time together."

Finally, Connie says, "I praise the Lord that I personally no longer have concerns that I am still holding on to. I pray over my children, pray over whomever they're spending time with, and simply trust in the Lord. I know that whatever happens, no matter whose care they're in, will be used for God's good. My husband struggles with it, and I think that God has given me this peace so that I can balance him out, keep us calm, and be in prayer over them."

He Assures Us We Are Not Alone

Many single moms I know are concerned about how their children will be affected by the lack of a father's regular presence in their lives. Military wives worry about this as well because of their husbands' long deployments. But God not only *filters out* what can damage our kids, He also *fills in the gaps* when it comes to situations we wish our children had.

Kadee, a military wife you've heard from in earlier chapters, is raising three young girls in Okinawa, Japan, and her husband is often deployed for months at a time.

"As a military wife, I have to fill dual roles often and with that comes extra worries and concerns. There have been days when I didn't get dressed or leave the house because my husband was deployed and I just didn't want to face the world alone with three small children. But with all that being said, I've been so blessed and taken care of by God. He is there when I cry out because I'm fed up with my children fighting and not listening and throwing fits because they just want daddy. I have to make a daily effort to acknowledge that God cares for me and is there to take my burdens. It doesn't mean it's always easy, nor is it pretty, but in the end, I have a much bigger God than my worries, stress, and fears."

And my friend Dawn Marie Wilson has seen God's faithfulness in this way as well:

"When my grown sons were little boys, my biggest concern for them was that they wouldn't have enough 'daddy influence.' Their dad was gone all the time in ministry. But the Lord heard my prayers of concern, and my husband became a great 'long-distance dad.' He called constantly, checking up on the boys, counseling, and encouraging them.

"Even though my boys weren't orphans, my husband traveled so much in ministry that I needed encouragement that God would father my boys. And I found hope in Psalm 68:5, which says God is a father of the fatherless.

"That's a weird verse to apply to a family like ours. But I know it has encouraged some single moms, and for many years, I felt like a single mom. Also, because I had to stand in my husband's stead so much with my boys, I felt I needed lots and lots of wisdom so they would grow up to be strong, wise boys. I feared that they might grow up less than masculine. But, I didn't need to worry about that —God made them both strong men!"

When God Fills In the Gaps

I mentioned earlier that God can not only filter out the garbage our children have been exposed to, but He can also fill in the gaps of whatever they're missing, as He did with Kadee and Dawn Marie, who feared having their husbands gone often might negatively affect their children.

Kathleen, whose story started this chapter and who is dealing with raising her teenage and young adult children without their dad around, has already seen God begin to fill in the gaps that her children's father had left.

"I had a horrible situation happen to my seventeen-year-old daughter. Unbeknownst to me, she went to a party and was drinking. The police busted the party and she was told to call me. My cell phone was off and she could not reach me or her dad. She finally reached our oldest son and he drove to the party and picked her up. I woke up to see her and my oldest son standing in my bedroom.

"For the next forty-five minutes, my oldest son proceeded to tell her the things that could have happened to her, what he has seen and heard happened to others in the situation she was in, and why it was wrong to do what she did.

"I truly know and believe that God had His hand in this situation. I always have my phone on, she knows that I am always there for her, and for the first time ever, she could not reach me.

"Yet God put my oldest son there to talk to her about the realities of underage drinking and what could have happened. It was so much more effective coming from her brother who was in college than from me.

"And, God protected her from anything bad happening and woke me up to the reality of my daughter drinking."

Kathleen said this situation not only gave her peace, since her daughter got a good lecture from her brother about drinking before going off to college, but has also helped deepen the relationship between her daughter and herself.

Kathleen is now convinced that God will be there to fill in the gaps in various ways that she feared would remain void when her husband left.

"I now take it step by step and day by day along with a God who loves me and has promised to never leave me," Kathleen said. "As hard as it is to trust God, I know He has a plan and purpose for my life—and theirs. Through this painfully difficult time, I have gotten to know the Lord like I never would have otherwise."

Trusting God's Filter

How have all these moms trusted God's filter? They found promises and guidelines in God's Word to hold onto, to pray over their children, to memorize, and to keep them strong. They also had a plan to not pass on fear to their children. As you go through the steps in this plan below, praise the Lord for being your sun and shield, and thank Him for the assurance "no good thing does he withhold from those whose walk is blameless" (Psalm 84:11).

Putting It into Practice

Trusting God's Faultless Filter

Here are some ways you can trust God's filter when something happens that you wish hadn't, when you're afraid that a wound of yours might be repeated in your children's lives, or when fear takes over.

Step 1: Take Your Insecurities, Disappointments, and Failures to God

Kathleen cited 1 Peter 5:7 as a huge comfort to her when she realized her children are now the victims of divorce: "Cast all your anxiety on him because he cares for you."

"This is so encouraging as a child of God because He cares about everything that concerns me, and He wants me to take it all to Him. If He cares about me, then He certainly cares about my kids. He's a good God, so I need to trust Him at all times—good and bad."

What cares, anxieties, or just plain disappointments do you need to cast on God so you can experience His peace as He filters out the garbage or fills in the gaps? List those cares here:

Step 2: Talk to Your Children About Boundaries

Marilyn set a boundary of no sleepovers for her children. And Angela felt confident about the boundaries she put around her daughter's mind by instructing her "If in doubt, call mom." She noticed that because of that instruction, her child was able to construct her own boundaries as she became an adult.

List here the boundaries you have thought about putting in place for your child, but haven't yet (or the ones that need to be reintroduced or reinforced):

Step 3: Teach Your Children by Example

Connie says, "This concept of modeling behavior to my children has sometimes been the most difficult thing to do, and it stops me in midsentence to think about what I say to them. It stops me in my tracks to choose a better response or reaction. It also humbles me as I turn to my two- or three-year-old daughter and confess my sin and ask for forgiveness over how I've acted. I have seen how she's transitioned to wanting to do things like me (she's always been all about Papa), so it encourages me to stay on track. It has changed me and helped me in my struggle to not react with anger and impatience."

What do your children need to see from you right now that will help them learn by example? Pray about this and record your answers here:

Step 4: Teach Your Children to Pray

No matter how young or old your children are, when you pray with them and teach them to pray themselves, you are investing in their spiritual life.

Gail Showalter, who founded an organization for single moms (SMORE), says, "There is really so very little that we control and yet as mothers we tend to think that we ought to control all aspects of our child's life. My most important prayer for my children was that *they pray.* Teaching children to worship and to pray not only takes away some of the mom's worry, but places the burden where it belongs—on the One who has the power to take care of them. One of the joys of being a mature mother is that I can see the fruit of having grown children who are certainly not without troubles, but who all (honor God) and are teaching their children to pray."

What is one tangible way that you can teach your child to pray, or remind them that you are praying for them? Do it this week.

. . . .
Becoming a Worry-Free Mom
—in Community
. . . .

For Thought or Discussion: Which of the four steps on pages 131-33 do you most need to work on? Share with others in your group how they can help you in incorporating any of those steps.

1. Review the stories of Joseph and Moses on pages 122-25. Which aspects of these stories are most reassuring to you? (circle any that apply, or add one of your own):

   • God's direction and presence in their lives, in spite of their surroundings.

   • God's promotion of each of these young individuals to a position of great influence.

   • God didn't allow the "baggage" from their past to dictate their future.

- Their commendable faith, despite their unfortunate circumstances.

- _____

2. Read the following passages of Scripture and record your reminder about how God is able to filter the garbage or fill in the gaps.

   Psalm 3—

   Psalm 7:10—

   Psalm 18:30—

   Psalm 18:35—

   Psalm 28:7—

   Proverbs 2:7—

3. Which of the above verses will you write out on a note card, put in front of you or carry with you, and commit to memorizing by next week? Write it out here to help you remember it:

4. Break into groups of two or three and pray together the following prayer, inserting the names of each other's children into this prayer:

Thank You, Lord Jesus, that You illumine our path and protect us on it as well. And You do the same with our children. Thank You that You will not withhold any good thing from _____ as _____ walks blamelessly (Psalm 84:11). I praise You, too, that You will not allow anything to touch _____'s life that hasn't first passed through Your loving hands. I trust in that. I rest in that. And I rest in You. Amen.

You Did What?

Secret 7: Giving Their Poor Decisions to God

*J*oani and her husband have been in ministry all their married lives. Their three children have grown up in the church, and all profess a love for the Lord. So I admire Joani's reaction when her oldest son, now 19, recently admitted to her that he had tried smoking pot at a friend's house.

Instead of responding by saying "You did *what?*" (as I might have), the panic in her heart didn't show in her voice or on her face. Instead of reacting emotionally, defensively, or accusingly, she calmly asked, "Wow, what made you want to do that?"

Taylor said that because his friends were always talking about it, he wanted to try it too.

"Do you think you'll want to do this again?" she asked.

"Maybe...but probably not," Taylor responded.

Then Joani proceeded to instruct her son: "You know, when something like this happens, it's a good opportunity to say, 'Hey, I tried it and now I know I don't want to continue this.' So I'm glad you tried it if it helped you arrive at that decision. And, if you claim to be a believer in Jesus, it's the type of behavior that probably isn't the best; it doesn't make you any less of a believer, it's just that you have the chance to be *all* His or have one foot in. It's ultimately *your* choice where you want to be with God."

Taylor's confession became a teaching moment for him. And

since then, he hasn't been afraid to come to his mom about other issues. (And he hasn't wanted to smoke pot again, either.)

I've known Joani's boys for years. And my response, upon hearing her story, was that if Joani and Mike had to deal with such issues, then any of us could find ourselves in similar situations. Even when we raise our kids in the church, even when we raise *really* good kids, things like this still happen. There's still temptation in this world. There are still times when our children don't make the best of choices. And there are always opportunities for teaching moments, rather than worry and grief.

Our Expectations

When we raise our children in church and give them a good solid biblical foundation at home, we tend to think that we'll never have to deal with situations like drugs, illegal drinking, pornography, promiscuity, or our children getting in trouble with the law. But in reality, our children, believers or not, are just as susceptible to the temptations of this world as anyone else. They will want to "try new things." They will disappoint us, probably many times, with their foolish choices.

Perhaps your heart has already been broken—from a lie your three-year-old told you, or the report about your child—cheating on a test, or the night your teenager didn't come home, or the day you learned your son was looking at porn. Your heart *will* break now and then because each of us, our kids included, have a sin nature. The Bible tells us in Romans 3:23, "All have sinned and fall short of the glory of God."

If our children have not claimed to be believers in Jesus Christ, then there can't be an expectation on our part for them to follow spiritual laws. Until they make a decision to live for Christ and have the indwelling Holy Spirit and a new nature, they will allow the world to be more influential in their lives.

Once they become believers, we can then shift our role to discipling them and helping them understand, as Joani did, what it means to be "all in" with God, or have just one foot in His camp and one foot in the world.

Yet even as committed followers of Christ, our children will still give in to temptation at times. I believe that the key to whether they will obey God or make poor decisions comes down to their relationship with God and whether they yield to the convicting the Holy Spirit does in their hearts. Yet another factor can be how we, as moms, respond to their rebellion. Will we overreact? Will we become judgmental? Will we try to clamp down and stir within them a desire to rebel even more? I believe our reaction will determine whether (1) they make that same bad decision again, or (2) they ask our advice when they are struggling with a temptation or choice.

The Reality of Rebellion

When our children make wrong choices, we may fear it reflects badly on us. And yet a pastor friend of mine told me something that profoundly impacted my thinking: "God was the perfect parent and Adam and Eve still sinned."

Think about that. God is absolutely perfect. He has no baggage or dysfunction from how He was "raised." He has no marriage difficulties for His children to deal with. He wasn't a workaholic who neglected His kids. And besides being perfect, He placed Adam and Eve in the perfect environment and provided them with everything they could possibly need and want to be happy for all eternity. God put them in a safe place, and clearly communicated the boundaries. (What good parent doesn't give their kids boundaries?) God drew the line at the "tree of the knowledge of good and evil." He didn't want them to know evil. He wanted them to remain innocent, in righteousness, in perfect unity with Him.

But Eve was curious, wasn't she? And Adam gave in to the "girl pressure," didn't he? These two people had absolutely perfect parenting, and they still chose poorly. Did that make God negligent, naïve, clueless, foolish, uninvolved, or just a bad parent? No. It means His children chose their way over His, and they paid the price for it.

So will our kids.

At one time or another, our children too will be curious about sin. They will see it as more desirable than doing what's right. They too will be tempted to test the limits. They too will lie, steal a piece of candy, or do something you clearly instructed them not to do. And when they do, you have a living reminder of why we need a Savior.

Your children's sin nature is bound to show itself sooner or later. When it does, you have an opportunity to talk to them about the new nature Christ offers. Or you can worry and panic and lose your cool. One key to successfully navigating your child's poor decisions, rebellion, or out-of-control thinking and behavior is how you respond.

Choosing How to Respond

Joani noticed that the pot-smoking incident, along with a beer-drinking incident and a couple other situations with her boys in the next year or so, started out with a confession after-the-fact and eventually turned into situations in which her boys asked *her* advice before venturing into something they were thinking about. Had Joani and Mike overreacted to the situations or thrown up their hands and said, "What's next?" or personalized each incident and defensively asked, "Why are you doing this to us?" they might have lost their sons' trust in them.

Instead, Joani's two sons learned that it was better to come to Mom and tell her what they were *thinking* of doing than break her heart by letting her find out on her own, or after the fact. And with their honesty and forewarning, Joani could have reacted emotion-ally and adamantly and said, "Absolutely not." But had she reacted that way, it's very possible her boys would've (1) gone ahead and done it anyway, or (2) taken note of their mom's reaction and con-cluded, "That's the last time we'll tell Mom what we have in mind." Instead, this wise mom said, on occasion, "It's your choice, but *know* that there just may be a consequence."

In short, Joani's boys learned, in hindsight, that their mom has good, sound advice. And they know now to heed her warning or listen to her advice.

Inviting Their Trust

We want our kids to tell us what's going on in their lives. But if they believe we'll be defensive, angry, judgmental, or lecturing, they may just decide to do things behind our backs and figure, "What Mom doesn't know won't hurt her."

You and I both know that once we discover what we *didn't* know, it ends up hurting even more.

Joani says, "My boys know they can come to us because we won't shame them or overreact. And that is only because of the connec-tion Mike and I have with God at the helm.

"How can I not overreact, but ask questions calmly and with-out shaming them? I've given it time. I've waited to address it. I've prayed about it first, calmed down, and then talked when the time was right. When something has been sprung on me, because my beliefs are what they are, I've been able to remain composed. Hon-estly, deep inside, I'm overreacting...but it's not detected because of the restraint of the Holy Spirit in my life. If my kids never fail, then they will never know what it means to heal and choose Christ over all these things."

Although there have been the usual bumps in the road, Joani

says, "My three kids [she has a preteen daughter too] are all doing so well today. I believe it is because of these three things: (1) Connection personally to Christ through His Word and an awareness of His Holy Spirit in my own life (as well as their observance of this); (2) reminding myself that my kids are "on loan"—they are not mine, but God's, and I have the privilege of discipling them and helping them grow; and (3) this allows nonreactive parenting when the first two things are in place."

Joani added: "When my boys were about five and seven, I asked them, 'What is it that you like about Mommy, and what is it you don't like?' They told me what they liked, and they said what they *didn't* like was that 'look' on my face and 'tone' in my voice when I'm angry. I learned right then and there that our children are also here to help keep us accountable. It's not just a parent/child relationship and accountability, it's child of God/child of God. We help each other grow. I told them that day, 'I will try to work on that. That is helpful information.' And, you know, that is where my desire began to build up my kids and create a safe environment where they are free to be honest. We really *can* talk about everything. It makes for a rich and rocky ride."

Joani realizes that her boys are still growing up, and she says, "I know that the days ahead may be rough, but I'm not worried." Her boys know God and know there are consequences to disobeying Him, and that there are blessings with obedience. "This world is not our home. It's not only a testing ground full of temptation, but a practice ground for love and acceptance!"

How Will You Respond?

How do you react when you hear that your child is making a poor decision? Do you worry and imagine the worst? Or do you take the matter to God in a missile prayer? My two favorite missile prayers are "Lord, help me to know how to react in this moment," and "God, please give me Your words, not mine."

We can push our children away with how we respond to their poor choices. Or we can draw them closer and teach them how to receive grace and learn from their mistakes. It all depends on whether you worry or exercise wisdom. Whether you panic or pray. Whether you are a worrier or a warrior. A worrier is one who dwells on the "What if…?" scenarios and constantly pictures her child ending up behind bars or living on the streets. A warrior is one who storms the gates of hell to remind the enemy, in Jesus' name, who that child really belongs to.

Worrier or Warrior?

Take a look at this chart below. If you are a worrier, your responses will reflect those on the left side, rather than the right:

A Worrier Thinks (or Says Aloud):	A Warrior Prays or Says:
What will this lead to?	This is something you can learn from.
Why would you do this to me?	This is not about me; this is about my child's heart.
What will other people say?	God, this is about You and my child.
Your chances at a great life are over now.	God forgives and restores and gives you another chance.

Where did you learn that kind of behavior?	We have all sinned, myself included. But this does not define you.
I'll let your dad (coach, principal, boss) deal with you.	I'm glad you came to me and confessed. (Or, if they didn't confess: Would you like me to pray with you about this?)

Can you see how the reactions in the left column imply that you are panicked, confused, or defensive? (The last response is even passive-aggressive.) No child wants to tell his mom or dad what he did when those kinds of emotional reactions inevitably follow. But if you are a warrior, your response will sound similar to those on the right side. They will be more prayerful, carefully thought out, and worded in a way that shows an understanding of the big picture, which is God's ultimate work in your child's heart. Also, by being a prayer warrior, you are calling upon the power of God to help you, whereas a worrier believes she is alone in the situation.

While there is a place for personal confrontation and exhortation, there is also a time and place for grace. If your child confessed to you, he or she is probably looking for that grace. If you happened to find out about their poor decision on your own, I strongly encourage you to take it to God first and ask Him for wisdom in how to respond. This test can be a teaching moment if you handle it correctly.

I believe that many times there is more benefit in talking to God *about* our children than in talking to our children about God (especially in moments of stress or discipline). Your children don't want a lecture when they already know their actions were wrong and they messed up. What they might need more is to see that you respond similarly to how God responds when we confess our sins to Him. When we disappoint God, He doesn't come unglued. He doesn't accuse further. He doesn't ignore us and make us earn the right to talk to Him again. He doesn't hold a grudge. And He doesn't lecture.

Psalm 103:8-14 describes our Heavenly Father's response toward us, and I believe it is a great model for how we should respond to our children, especially when they are repentant:

> The LORD is compassionate and gracious,
>   slow to anger, abounding in love.
> He will not always accuse,
>   nor will he harbor his anger forever;
> he does not treat us as our sins deserve
>   or repay us according to our iniquities.
> For as high as the heavens are above the earth,
>   so great is his love for those who fear him;
> as far as the east is from the west,
>   so far has he removed our transgressions from us.
>
> As a father has compassion on his children,
>   so the LORD has compassion on those who fear him;
> for he knows how we are formed,
>   he remembers that we are dust.

And in Isaiah 43:25 we learn that God chooses not to remember our offenses, and will never bring them up again:

> I, even I, am he who blots out your transgressions,
>   for my own sake,
>   and remembers your sins no more.

Can you be a compassionate, loving, patient parent like that, even in light of your child's offenses? That is my goal, and I'm sure it's yours too.

Replacing Panic with Peace

I know that you, like me, don't want to be a mom who panics and reacts emotionally when she finds out her children have messed up. So here are some words of advice that Joani and other moms have given, as well as wisdom from God's Word, to help us display peace rather than panic when our children let us down.

Dwell on the Best, Not the Worst

What will you do with the information you have about a poor choice your child has made? Will you use it to become paranoid that your child is even worse than he or she admitted? Will you begin to suspect their wrongdoing at every turn? A worrier continues to dwell on the worst that might happen. But a warrior dwells on the best, and takes that to God in prayer.

Remember that formula for peace in Philippians 4:6-8 that we talked about in chapter 2? It is also a formula for a wise response to your children's sin: (1) Worry about nothing; (2) pray about everything; (3) think on what is true; and (4) experience God's peace.

To think on what is true is to dwell on the best that God is capable of accomplishing, not the worst that could occur. During my daughter's early teenage years, I was so afraid of being clueless about my daughter's involvements that I actually became a bit paranoid that she might be keeping something from me. My friends were telling me stories, left and right, of things their children were doing behind their backs, and I didn't want to be the naïve mom who just assumed my daughter never did anything like that.

But looking back now, why not? If I was worried about being naïve, the focus was on *me*...and how I looked. I had a daughter who was not bent on rebellion. She was not the secretive type. She was forthright and honest in most cases. And although we had our situations, on occasion, when she was younger and not completely honest with me, she wasn't sneaking or conniving or doing *any* of what I feared she was. I now wish that I had trusted her and given her the benefit of the doubt. I wish I'd focused on the best in her, rather than the "What if…?"

In Psalm 139:17-18, David the psalmist said God thinks only the best about us: "How precious also are Your thoughts to me, O God! How great is the sum of them!" (NKJV).

God doesn't just have *lots* of thoughts about us, but they are *precious* thoughts. Thoughts that are good, kind, and loving, even though He knows perfectly well what we are capable of. God's thoughts of us are not based on ignorance of what we're doing, but on the picture of how He sees us—pure and spotless when we are trusting in His Son, Jesus, for our righteousness and salvation. God thinks the best about us even when He truly knows the worst about us.

Can you think about your child the way God thinks about you?

Distinguish Between Fear and Discernment

I had a friend years ago who would often have nightmares about the safety or behavior of her middle-school-aged son. "I'm so fearful something is going to happen to him," she would say to me. "I think God is telling me to pray for him so this doesn't happen."

And yet Scripture says, "God has not given us a spirit of fear" (2 Timothy 1:7 NKJV). Fear is imagining the worst. Fear is a lack of trust. Fear is the absence of faith.

God doesn't give you dreams to make you fearful. Nor will He let you know something is about to happen, unless He accompanies it with perfect peace. God is the One who gives peace in the face of fear. He is the One who prepares your heart with calm, not panic, if something is about to happen.

God may, on the other hand, impress upon your heart to pray for a child in the middle of the night, only to find out later that was the time when he or she needed help or was in a potentially dangerous situation. But that pressing on your heart to pray will not be fear—only concern or a sense of urgency to pray. (You'll read more about this kind of scenario in the next chapter.)

Don't Worry About What Others Will Think

A friend who has three grown children recently told me: "It's usually in the middle of the night that I begin to worry about my children...when I begin dwelling on the things I think they should be doing or areas I think need improvement. So often I want to be in control of their actions. And to be honest, many times my worry stems from fear of what others will think of my children and me as their parent. Over and over, I have to practice voicing all my fears to God and coming back to reason, looking at situations from His perspective and remembering that each of my children is a work in progress with God, just as I am."

When we realize we are accountable to God—not others—for how we raise our children, we can rest more easily in the fact that God understands, even if others misunderstand.

Don't Give Up on Them

The Bible's description of love in 1 Corinthians 13:4-7 is often read at weddings and held up as a model for godly love between a husband and wife. But this picture of godly love applies to the parent-child relationship as well. Note especially the last verse in this passage:

> Love is patient, love is kind. It does not envy, it does not boast, it is not proud. It does not dishonor others, it is not self-seeking, it is not easily angered, it keeps no record of wrongs. Love does not delight in evil but

rejoices with the truth. It *always protects, always trusts, always hopes, always perseveres.*

In another translation, that last sentence says love "bears all things, believes all things, hopes all things, endures all things" (NASB).

Those four words—bears, believes, hopes, endures—describe what it truly means to not give up on our kids, but to parent them lovingly in spite of the problems.

Are you really bearing with your children in all things, believing the best about them in every situation, hoping for good in all they are involved in, and enduring all things with them? When you can say *yes* to all four, you are loving them as God loves you.

Extending Grace

When I was writing my book *When a Mom Inspires Her Daughter,* I interviewed several young women who were raised in Christian homes and believed their parents held a standard too high for them to meet. They described their upbringing using words like *legalistic, overbearing,* and *perfectionist.*

Now it's true that God holds a high standard for all of us. Yet absolutely none of us can meet that standard. That's why we needed Jesus' death on the cross to secure our forgiveness and righteousness before God and to stay our judgment over all we have been guilty of our entire lives. When we begin to see our children as sinners, just as we are, and people who need grace and forgiveness just like we do, it will help us respond to them in a much more loving and Christlike way.

We *all* are a work in progress. All of us moms. And all of our children. We are all developing, stumbling (literally) through toddlerhood and (figuratively) through adolescence and adulthood. And God is working on our kids and on us at the same time in His own way. Trust the process—the physical growing-up process, and the spiritual growing-up process. God is making both you and your children into the people He wants each of you to become.

It's easy sometimes to stand in judgment of our children, to be harsh with them because we want to hold the line. To look down on them from our pillar of self-righteousness and talk down to them because of the messes they've made. Ultimately, however, it is love that always wins. Grace always rules. Love covers a multitude of sins (1 Peter 4:8). And love keeps the door open for restoration.

Love Them Like God Does

Finally, one of the reasons we worry is we tend to look at what might be, and what we should be preparing for, and we forget that God is working very much in the here and now, in our children's lives, as well as our own.

Oswald Chambers said, "God is not working toward a particular finish—His purpose is the process itself. It is the process, not the outcome, that is glorifying to God.

"God's training is for now, not later. His purpose is for this very minute, not for sometime in the future." That goes for your child as well as for you. Chambers observed, "If we realize that moment-by-moment obedience is the goal, then each moment as it comes is precious."[22]

Each moment is not only precious, but can be a teachable moment as well when you consider that God is at work now in the life of your child—in their good decisions *and* their bad ones, when they're delighting your heart and when they're breaking it.

Love them like God does throughout their offenses. And you may learn a lot about how God loves *you* as well.

Putting It into Practice

···

Giving Their Poor Decisions to God

Insert your children's names in the blanks below and pray this *for* them now—and *with* them when appropriate:

God, thank You that _____'s decisions never take You by surprise. And those decisions never lessen Your love for _____, either. Search _____, O God, and know his/her heart; test _____ and know his/her anxious thoughts. See if there is any offensive way in _____, and lead _____ in the way everlasting (Psalm 139:23-24). Broaden the path beneath _____, so that his/her ankles do not turn (Psalm 18:36). Give _____ understanding so that he/she will keep your law and obey it with all his/her heart. Direct _____ in the path of your commands, for there he/she will find delight. Turn _____'s heart toward your statutes and not toward selfish gain. Turn _____'s eyes away from worthless things; preserve _____'s life according to your word (Psalm 119:34-37). Above all else, guard _____'s heart, for it is the wellspring of life (Proverbs 4:23). Give me wisdom, as _____'s mom, to guide _____, to show grace toward him/her in the same way You do, and to show him/her, from my own life, what it means to have a closer, more obedient walk with You.

Becoming a Worry-Free Mom
—in Community

For Thought or Discussion: How do you respond or react when you discover your child has made a poor or foolish decision?

1. Looking at the chart on page 143-44, would you classify yourself as a worrier or a warrior? Why?

2. Which of the following is the most challenging for you right now?
   a) Dwell on the best in your child, not the worst
   b) Distinguish between fear and discernment
   c) Don't worry about you and your reputation
   d) Don't give up on them

   How can you glean help from God and others in that area?

3. Look up the following verses and record God's response to sin:
   Psalm 103:8—

   Psalm 103:9—

   Psalm 103:10—

Psalm 103:12—

Isaiah 43:25—

4. Which of the above verses will you print out and post on
   your refrigerator, computer desktop, or car dashboard
   so you can see them when you are tempted to react
   emotionally to a bad decision made by your child?

8

You're Breaking My Heart

Secret 8: Trusting God with Their Spiritual Foundation

How does a mom truly trust God and not worry when she sees her child start spiraling downward?

How does she know when to say something, and when to let her child work it out?

How can she trust that God ultimately has good in mind when it all looks so bad?

I asked my friend, Cyndie, to tell you her story in her own words so that you could relate to her mother's heart, feel her pain in her struggles, and rejoice with her at how God ultimately came through.

"Probably the most fearful time for me as a mom was watching my daughter completely change from a young woman who looked to God for every need to one on a path of self-destruction.

"She came to know the Lord at a very early age and lived her life with the sole purpose of serving Him. I remember watching her take her 'Wordless Book' outside and gather the neighborhood children together so that she could present the plan of salvation with it. She was only six years old. I smile when I remember the sweet little voice singing praise songs when she went to bed at night. God gave her a beautiful singing voice, which she used for His glory for many years.

"All through school she continued on her path toward Christian service. She was involved with many missions trips, retreats, and Bible study. She often prayed for friends who were struggling and reached out to others without concern about what it might cost her to do so, sometimes resulting in rejection and alienation from the very people she cared so much about.

"My daughter chose to attend a Christian college and excelled academically. However, personal relationships were still a struggle, and I could see that she appeared to be somewhat depressed. She decided to go and see a counselor with whom she worked for a short while. By the time she graduated, she had gained a substantial amount of weight and was still struggling with depression. After graduate school she went to work in a very stressful, high-responsibility job. It was no surprise that she did great; in fact, she is still with the same organization today. She was promoted often and continued to invest in the lives of others both at work and at church, always keeping her eyes on the Lord, seeking His guidance for her life."

The Unexpected Downward Spiral

"As the years passed, she continued to gain weight. After numerous failed weight loss programs and a lot of prayer, she decided to have gastric bypass surgery. It was successful and within the first year, she lost 130 pounds. She looked great and felt great. She seemed to be excited about life again, but she began to notice how differently she was treated by both men and women, and this bothered her. She would often say she was the same person she had always been, so why all the attention now? It was also at this time I sensed a struggle within her regarding church. She began to skip a Sunday here and there using work as the reason, and that may have been the case, but it was totally unlike her.

"She began to date for the first time, and then her job took her overseas for several months. It was there she received her first kiss. At the same time, she began to drink an occasional glass of wine. She was encouraged by a friend who told her it would help her to be less inhibited and better able to relax while on a date. Since she was in her thirties, she too thought it was time she grew up and experienced the dating life and all that went with it. This was alarming to me and I talked with her about it, but she assured me that it was not a problem. I was concerned, however, because I have a family history of alcoholism and mental illness. So to say I was alarmed is putting it mildly! Our lives were about to travel a road I *never* would have imagined we'd travel!

"I watched and prayed for many years as my beautiful daughter slowly spiraled out of control. I reached out to family and even her friends at times, hoping that someone would understand my concern and talk to her about what was happening in her life. For the most part I was told that I was overreacting and she was just "catching up," since she had not experienced the things many young people experience while in college and in young adulthood. I had so many conversations with her about this, mostly over the phone, and while we talked, she would be drinking wine. She frequently forgot our conversations, which gave me one more reason to fear that I might lose her.

"There were many nights I cried and pleaded with God to 'fix' my daughter. I told God I would do whatever I had to do to help her… but nothing happened, and with each new year of watching her self-destruct I was falling into my own depression, being led by fear and even anger and disappointment with God. I just couldn't come to terms with how God could let this child, His child, go down the road she was on when she had lived for Him for decades! I felt completely alone, sad, disappointed, and full of fear.

"I was unable to pray, but God, in His mercy and grace, still found ways to speak to me—whether through a thought that came to mind, a song on a Christian radio station, or even just one sentence in a message at church. I continued to read inspirational books and my

Bible, and I found strength and encouragement in them—enough to get me through one long night...to the next place in my journey.

Mom's Journey Too

"I didn't realize it at the time, but this was *my* journey as well. After about eight years of dealing with everything that goes with watching a child self-destruct, I decided I needed help trying to fig-ure it out. I sought out a Christian counselor, hoping that I could find some relief from what was now full-blown depression. My daughter came to a couple of sessions with me thinking that her input would be helpful in my healing process, which it was, but she had no idea how much of my pain resulted from her drinking and my fear for her well-being. As it turned out, she had a connection with the counselor and decided to go into therapy too.

"During the first year, every session for me was centered on my daughter. She was now drinking at least two bottles of wine every night and hadn't realized yet that this was a huge problem. I think I assumed that the drinking would stop right away and she would be the young woman I missed so much as soon as she began counsel-ing. But that didn't happen. I was afraid she would end up hurting herself, or worse. But one night God used a woman at church who was sharing her testimony to speak directly to me. I heard God say, through this woman, 'Cyndie, can you trust Me with your pain *even if* you never see the results you hope for?' Right then and there I got it. God is in control! My pain is my pain, and my daughter's pain is her pain. I can only be responsible for myself—that's it!"

Releasing the Burden

"At that moment of realization I finally gave my daughter back to God. He is the Father, not me! Such a burden was lifted from my shoulders, bringing a spiritual and emotional release I thought would never come. I realized that it wasn't my job to fix my daughter or anyone else. All the guilt I felt for 'not doing a good enough job' raising my daughter was unnecessary because she is an adult and makes her own choices. Do I wish I had done some things differently? Yes! Can I go back and change any of it? Of course not. But again, it's not for me to fix anybody; God can make a masterpiece out of the jumbled-up mess we often make of our lives. It was time for me to exercise a little faith. I finally felt safe with my heavenly Father. This was huge for me! I am a 'fixer,' and stepping back is one of the most difficult things I've had to learn and am still learning.

"There were several months after my daughter began counseling that she distanced herself from me. Evidently she felt some resentment, and the few times I talked to her on the phone I could hear the annoyance in her voice as well as an edge of hostility. This was so hard to deal with. My heart was broken, but God reminded me that I had given her to Him at whatever the cost to me, reminding me that He is enough.

"Our second year into counseling, my daughter began to rebuild her relationship with God. She started attending church again, and got involved with the singles ministry and Bible study. She also began softening toward me. She realized that alcohol was in fact destroying her life and she decided to quit drinking. She said she lost the desire immediately and doesn't find herself thinking about it at all, even when she's feeling upset or anxious. It has been two years since she drank last. She is rebuilding her relationship with God and letting herself 'feel' instead of numbing herself with alcohol. I'm so proud of the hard work she has put into the healing process. And I'm thankful to a God who loves us no matter what. My relationship with my daughter is much different today, and in a good way. We don't depend on each other to fix or heal our hurts; we take that to the Lord. This has allowed our relationship to move beyond one of codependence to mutual respect.

"It sounds so cliché, but there's truth to the saying 'let go and let

God.' I'm still learning this of course! I don't know if I'm a worry-free mom or not, but I'm able to be a better mom because I no longer try to guide a conversation to the place where I can make my point or try to manipulate her or my sons into making what I consider the right choice. I have the freedom to trust that I did the best job I could while raising them, knowing that in spite of being so young when I started [only 17], I still gave them all my love, stability, discipline, affection, and a pathway to Jesus—things I didn't experience while growing up.

"I'm so blessed and I'm thankful that God already knows my story and the stories of my children, that He has already "walked" where I am walking, and that He—and He alone—can comfort me when I'm drowning in a sea of pain and uncertainty. All my worrying is for naught! In fact, worry keeps me from a trusting relationship with my heavenly Father, and that is not the way I want to live my life any longer! I can hear Him whisper, 'Have faith, trust Me—I will carry you through every trial because you're My daughter and because I love you.'"

Today, Cyndie marvels at the complete restoration that God has done in her daughter's heart. God, in His mercy and grace, brought Cyndie's daughter back from a season of wandering in the dark. I say season because that's what it was. It's important for us to remember that often it's a season. And it's in that time that we have the opportunity to wait upon God and learn how to trust Him.

Our Broken Hearts

I discovered, when interviewing moms for this book, that one of the most intense concerns a mother has for her children is for their spiritual condition. We fear our children will turn their backs on their faith and all they were taught and needlessly stumble through life.

That situation can not only be fearful, but it can make us feel so helpless.

So many of the moms I interviewed for this book are strong women of faith. They have raised their children to be churchgoing, Bible-believing, Jesus-loving individuals. But some of their children chose a different road. Some of these moms, like Cyndie, have seen God direct those children back to the God of their youth. Others, however, still continue to pray and hold out for what they know God is doing in their lives and the lives of their children.

Barbara is one such mom. Her son, now 20, is in a vulnerable spot, and all she can do is pray for him.

"My son had a strong upbringing in the Word of God," Barbara said. "At one time he had a passion to be a youth pastor, but he strayed into the ways of the world and got mixed up with drugs, alcohol, and the police. He has completed rehab and now has his first steady job."

And yet he is daily on her heart and in her prayers.

"My concerns for him overwhelm me almost daily," she said. "My first and primary concern is that he finds his way back to the God who has never left his side. I also hope and pray he will stay strong in his ability to say *no* to the world that tries so hard to drag him back down, and that he sees in himself the man whom God sees—one who was created to serve and glorify Him."

What About That Verse?

I know what you're thinking about now. Doesn't the Bible promise that if you raise a child in the right way, he will not depart from it?

Many moms grab onto Proverbs 22:6 ("Train up a child in the way he should go, even when he is old he will not depart from it" NASB) and claim it as their promise or guarantee that if they raise their kids in Sunday school or teach them biblical principles when they're young, their children will not turn their backs on their faith. But it's important to understand that Scripture contains specific promises, and it also contains general principles for life. This verse in Proverbs is a principle or guideline, like many of the wise sayings of Solomon, that "if you do this, chances are this other thing will happen."

I know of parents who start their children in the ways and Word of God who never see their children return. That is where we trust God's work in their lives. That is where we trust that God sees what we cannot see. That is where we trust that God will take what we have done to honor Him and work it for good in their lives.

The wording in that verse—"even when he is old he will not depart from it"—could mean that *when your child is old* he will return to his childhood faith. It could mean, mom, that you won't see it happen in your lifetime. It could mean a deathbed conversion for your son or daughter, or a repentance and coming back to the faith of their childhood when their life is nearly over. That certainly is not what any of us desires. But again, there is peace when we trust the wisdom, goodness, and timing of God to guide our children with what we have given them.

Instead of relying on Proverbs 22:6 as a "guarantee" that my child will be okay, I find greater hope in Hebrews 13:5, which reminds us that God will never leave us or forsake us. If our children have made sincere commitments to Christ at some point in their lives, and there was evidence of the Holy Spirit working in them, manifesting a changed life, then we have hope that those children are not truly lost in terms of salvation, but have just, like sheep, gone astray. Our assurance, in that case, is that God has promised to never leave them. Jesus said in John 10:28 that "no one will snatch them out of My hand" (NASB). Furthermore, Romans 8:38-39 tells us that nothing will be able to separate us (or our believing children) from the love of God. Now those are lifelines worth holding onto.

What I appreciate the most about those verses is that, unlike Proverbs 22:6, the weight of responsibility in those verses is on *God*, who keeps His promises—not on us and how good of a job we did or didn't do in raising our children.

Do you know what that means? It means regardless of our efforts or worries, God is the One who can keep our children in His hand or turn their hearts back toward Him in His own way and His own time.

Peggy's Concerns

Peggy, a mom of two children now in their thirties, said she too worried about her son's relationship with God, which turned to rebellion.

"I was worried about my son when he was away from God and making wrong choices. While he was in the Navy, he became depressed and went AWOL. We talked to him many times on the phone. We encouraged him and prayed for him. He also had a Christian girl waiting for him. He finally did what was right and turned himself in and began to trust God for the outcome. The Lord worked in his life. He came home and began going to church again. The Lord totally turned his life around. My prayer was for my son to remember that he belonged to God, and that he would turn back to Him. I prayed that God would bring him out of the depression. I knew that God had His hand on my son and would not let him go. It was a difficult time. I wasn't always trusting, but when I did, God gave me peace."

Peggy also recalls that as she remembered to apply Philippians 4:6-7 to her life—that is, not worry, but pray and focus on what was right and true—she experienced God's peace.

When It Seems Like God's Not There

If your child is living a lifestyle in which he or she appears to have no acknowledgment of God, you might be thinking God has dropped them like they appear to have dropped God. But God hasn't dropped them. Furthermore, if you're not sure whether your child ever did know and follow God, it's a fact that God will never drop *you*. And sometimes He is doing a transforming work in you as you pray in the midst of your child's rebellion.

If you raised or are raising your child in the ways of the Lord and that child is rebelling, I know you are experiencing heartache. There are times you will not see the resolution of your child's rebellion or addiction, but you *will* see glimpses of God's care and whispers of His love along the way if you stay sensitive to His Spirit's leading in how to pray and how to act.

Janice (not her real name) has four living children, two of them disabled. She has also lost two other children. It would be in her nature to worry. But she has learned through the years that her Father can be trusted with the things she cannot control—the loss of a child, as well as the heartache that comes from having a wayward child.

I will let her tell you how God worked in what appeared to be a hopeless situation.

"Our daughter was heavily into drugs during her high school years and when she was a freshman in college. She did whatever she needed to get them. One weekend we could not find her.

"We were ready to walk out the door to go to church when, simultaneously, my husband and I said, "Let's go look for her." We traveled into the worst sections of the city, driving up one street and down the other. Then we spotted her car.

"I thanked God for directing us to her. But which boarded-up house was she in? We took different sides of the street and knocked on many doors. Can you picture this? My husband in a suit and tie, myself in heels and pearls. What were we thinking? We should have changed clothes when we decided to go look for her instead of going to church, but we didn't. God had a plan even in that.

"Finally one door opened. I asked if my daughter was there or if this woman knew her. She looked me up and down and then told me I did not belong in this part of town. She said she had answered the door only because I looked nice and she knew no cop would look like I did. She told me she had seen our daughter and she believed she was 'over there.' She pointed to a boarded-up house across the street. Every window and door had boards nailed across it.

"We went over to that house and banged on every piece of plywood. There was no answer. Our hands were sore and my husband's knuckles were bleeding. All we could do was pray. I left a tear-soaked note on my daughter's windshield:

> Dear Squeaks,
>
> We love you very much. God loves you greater still. Please come home.
>
> Love, Mom and Dad xxoo

"My husband and I cried all the way home. We looked and felt so out-of-place in that area we were in."

Yet God was right there with those two heartsick parents—through every knock on every piece of wood. And He heard their pleas—and caused their daughter to hear them too.

"We learned later that the cries of her mother and father calling out her name on the street made our daughter realize that she was loved. She was in a drugged stupor, but she was alert enough to hear her name and the voices of her parents. I believe it was our Heavenly Father who intervened and spared all of us a horrific end."

Janice recalls another time that God woke her up at 1:00 a.m.

to pray for her daughter. So she was awake and praying when the phone rang in her home at 1:30 a.m.

"The police officer wanted to know why I did not sound sleepy. I told him that God had awakened me to pray for my daughter. I then asked him if she was okay. It took him back that I was so calm when I asked and heard his response. It was my Father who had prepared me. On our way to the jail that early morning it was still dark and a deer ran in front of our car. All I could think of was 'As the deer pants for the water brooks, so pants my soul for You, O God' [Psalm 42:1 NKJV]. The song set to that Scripture verse filled my heart with comfort."

Janice saw that incident as God telling her to keep her eyes and heart fixed on Him.

"When we arrived at the jail, I was relieved that we happened to have some emergency cash in our house. I had grabbed it and my husband grabbed the checkbook when we left to go to the jail cell. Jails take cash only, so we had what we needed to bring her home that night."

When Janice had no hope left that her daughter would make a change for the better, she put her hope in God and who He is. Change didn't happen immediately, but God eventually brought Janice's daughter back to her senses, back to her family, and back to Himself. Today, Janice's daughter is married with three children, and is "a wonderful, amazing mom who loves the Lord and serves Him with gladness," Janice said.

I've asked hundreds of moms to share with me their secrets to maintaining hope for a wayward child, even when the situation looks hopeless. Their answer is always the same. Their hope is in God, not their child, and God's ability to turn that child's heart back toward home.

Our Hope During Heartache

Who raises a child to turn to drugs? None of us. Who imagines their child will lead a destructive life? Not you or me. And yet not one of our child's decisions or actions takes God by surprise. In order to get through their little lies and foolish decisions, as well as their dangerous acts of rebellion, we have to be firmly grounded in God's Word and His character and the fact that He can get us—and our children—safely through.

Seek Comfort in God's Word

Janice says her only comfort during the season of her daughter's rebellion was praying Scripture over her daughter. Isaiah 49:16 was especially encouraging to her: "See, I have engraved you on the palms of my hands; your walls are ever before me."

While that verse prophetically refers to the nail prints in Jesus' hands, it symbolizes to us that Jesus knew each and every person by name, that He would die for and those nail prints were like an engraved name on His hand.

"What a comfort to know that my daughter's name was engraved in Jesus' hands," Janice said. "She had received the Lord as her Savior when she was seven years old. But there were so many things she had to deal with in her young life that by the time she was fourteen, it all came to a head. She had lost a sister, she had two disabled siblings. She herself suffered with juvenile rheumatoid arthritis. Her spirit had enough and her mother was too busy handling her disabled brothers to notice all her pain. Oh, but God is merciful and full of unfailing love toward us."

Barbara, whose son went AWOL, said she has also found comfort in God's Word, especially the verses that talk about His character.

"The scripture I have prayed most over my son is Psalm 139—what peace knowing that God is there with him in the dark, in the light, waking up, going to sleep, going out, coming in."

Do you realize, just from Psalm 139 alone, we learn that God is One who

- searches us and knows us from the inside out (verse 1)
- knows our every action and thought (verses 2-3)
- knows what we will say before we say it (verse 4)
- follows us everywhere we go (verses 8-12)
- formed us and watched over us while we were in the womb (verses 13-15)
- wrote out our life story in His book before we even lived it (verse 16)
- thinks innumerable thoughts of us (verses 17-18)
- knows our anxieties (verse 23)
- convicts us of our offenses and leads us in the right direction (verse 24)

That psalm reminds us that God is more intimately acquainted with our child than we will ever be. And that He is tracking their whereabouts when we can't. Considering that God is able to do all of that, there isn't a reason to worry, is there? Keep reminding yourself of who God is. Highlight those passages. Write them on cards you can place wherever you will see them several times throughout the day. Say them aloud. And be comforted by the all-knowing, all-powerful, ever-present character of God.

Stay Tuned to the Spirit's Voice

Janice said she would have missed God's guiding voice if she hadn't been in a state of continual prayer and intercession for her daughter. As she struggled with not knowing where her daughter was, God continually impressed upon her heart how to pray, when to pray, and where to look. We can stay tuned to the Holy Spirit's voice by being in God's Word daily and maintaining an attitude of prayer and reliance on God's help so we can pick up on His "cues" when He gives them.

Submit to Him in Worship

Lisa remembers the day she was at her wits' end with her oldest son, Dustin.

As she watched him spiral downward, she learned two things: God is faithful, and her response to Him needed to be nothing short of worship:

"My oldest son's addictions had taken him to the brink and my emotions followed. It was out of my hands, and I had to give him over to God. The despair was overwhelming and the enemy wanted me to believe death would be the only cure. But not so with God. Although there was going to be much more chaos to ensue (an auto accident that would put my son in the hospital; he would go to rehab only to relapse, and he would be allowed to go 'crazy' for three days before God crashed in), there was one thing God was calling me to do—worship.

"I had no words; only tears. My fears wanted to immobilize me and God wanted to free me. I made my way out to the front yard to a palm tree where I sat and I cried. Only the Holy Spirit could interpret what I was trying to pray aloud. Worship began to overflow from the very core of my being. I didn't want to stop; it felt so safe there. God's presence was with me and He understood everything I was feeling and all I did and would continue to go through... Was I willing to surrender all so that God could do a greater work? I wanted my will and my heart to come into alignment with His.

Even if my son's choices would take him from me, I wanted to be a woman who worshipped God regardless of the circumstances."

What God did in Dustin's life was amazing, Lisa said.

"My heart cries with joy and awe every time I think or speak of him. He is now living a responsible life as a productive citizen, husband, and father. What God can do is above and beyond what we could ever imagine or hope for. God had a plan for Dustin. When Dustin stopped in the midst of madness and asked Him what the plan would be, I don't think he ever imagined the goodness that would stem from that one request. Dustin is simply catching his breath for all that God has done!"

Lisa rejoices today as Dustin's season of rebellion and life-threatening addiction is now a story of God's deliverance, rather than one of his demise.

Love Them Home

Over the years, I have criticized child celebrities gone bad in front of my daughter and I have, regrettably, sounded judgmental. Dana, who loved some of these individuals when they were in their prime, has often responded more compassionately by saying, "Mom, she's just really confused right now" or "Mom, she's just lost her way." I think Dana's right. Many of these childhood celebrities grow up and lose their way, as we all do, at times.

Jesus said we *all* like sheep have gone astray. We check out other pastures. We wander off, not realizing how far we've gone until we look around and realize we're lost and there are wolves lurking in the bushes, waiting to devour us. We then want to come back to the safety and security of the fold, but what will await us when we return?

Jesus told a story in Luke 15 that we have come to know as the parable of the prodigal son. But I think that story is mislabeled. It is much more about the compassionate father. In this story, a father's youngest son asks for his share of the family inheritance early. (In Jewish culture, that was like saying to your father, "I wish you were dead.") This father gave his son his share of the inheritance, and the son went to a far country and squandered all his riches on foolish living. He ended up being a hired hand starving and sleeping with pigs (a rock-bottom situation for a Jewish man). When this young man came to his senses, he decided to go back home and offer himself as a servant laborer so he could at least have a few meals each day. But the wayward son's father (who represents our heavenly Father), responded to his son's rebellion and return in a most surprising way:

1. He *watched* the road—perhaps daily—hoping for his child's return.

2. He was *filled with compassion* upon seeing his son, *ran* to meet him, threw his arms around him, and kissed him.

3. He *celebrated* his child's return by throwing him a party fit for a king.

This father actually *longed* for his rebellious son's return, rather than thinking, *That boy better never show his face around here again.* Then when he saw his son in the distance, he was filled with compassion. This wise father knew his son—approaching with head down, ashamed, dirty—had already suffered the consequences of his foolishness. He was already humiliated. He had already paid the price for his rebellion. At this point he desperately needed to be loved. So his father laid aside his dignity, picked up the robe around his feet, and *ran* to meet his son. I'm so glad to learn the father wasn't prideful and thinking, *I'll let him approach, say his apologies, and then I'll decide how to best deal with his actions.* Instead, he couldn't wait to embrace his son. And then, even more unexpected and downright outlandish—with no regard for what the rest of the family or neighborhood would say—he threw a *party* in his son's honor!

You and I have a Daddy like that. A Daddy who parties upon His wayward child's return. So can you and I be a *mommy* like that? One who runs to meet our wayward child at the first sign of repentance? One who throws a party when they've come home? There will be some who will be critical and won't understand (like the older son, who resented all the fuss his rebellious-turned-repentant brother was receiving). And culturally, others would have expected that father to preserve his dignity and keep his distance. But the father had the right perspective. It was his child. It was his heart coming back home.[23]

My prayer is that if the time ever comes that your rebellious child returns in repentance, you will be the parent who drops your pride and parties upon his or her return. All heaven will be doing the same.[24]

Time to Trust

As we surrender our children to God, we can trust that they are in His hands and He'll do whatever work He wants to do in them, and in us, for His glory. We can worry, or we can pray. We can stress, or we can trust. We can lose sleep by trying to control their every step. Or we can rest in the One who is already in control of their lives whether they are acting like it or not.

Putting It into Practice
....
Trusting God with Their Spiritual Life

Here is how you can surrender and trust God with your children's spiritual lives:

Step 1: Pray for your child to discern God's voice

Jamie, a mom of six kids, says "I always pray for God to be loud to them."

Children will hear our voice in their heads. And they may try to shut out that voice at times if their hearts are hardened. Children will also hear their friends' and peers' voices, and the voice of the enemy seeking to lead them astray. And we want God's voice—the voice of His Holy Spirit—to be louder than anyone else's voice.

Insert your child's name in this prayer and pray it often:

"Lord, help _____ to listen to what You say, and to treasure Your commands. Tune _____'s ears to wisdom, and help _____ concentrate on understanding (Proverbs 2:1-2 NLT). Instruct _____ in the way of wisdom and lead _____ along straight paths (Proverbs 4:11).

Step 2: Pray for wisdom to know when to speak and when to be silent

There will come a time when your words will fall on deaf ears, but God's never will. Pray for wisdom so you know when to speak, and when to be silent so *God* can speak. Here's a way to pray for that right now:

Lord, Your Word says, "If any of you lacks wisdom, he should ask God, who gives generously to all without finding fault, and it will be given to him" (James 1:5).

I need Your kind of wisdom so I know when to speak to _____ and when to be silent. "Do not let any unwholesome talk [lecturing, judging, or accusing] come out of [my] mouth, but only what is helpful for building [my children] up according to their needs, that it may benefit those who listen (Ephesians 4:29). Let me also be "quick to listen, slow to speak and slow to become angry, for [my] anger doesn't bring about the righteous life that God desires" (James 1:19).

Step 3: Praise God for what you don't yet see

First Thessalonians 5:16-18 clearly spells out God's will for you and me, as women, wives, moms, and children of God: "Be joyful always; pray continually; give thanks in all circumstances for this is God's will for you in Christ Jesus" (1 Thessalonians 5:16-18).

It couldn't be said any simpler:

- be joyful—always
- pray—continually
- thank God—for *all* circumstances, not just the ones you are comfortable with

Say (or write in the space below) a prayer thanking God now for something in your child's life that you wouldn't ordinarily be thankful for. Do this to show your trust in the work God is doing in your child's life.

Becoming a Worry-Free Mom
—in Community

For Thought or Discussion: What aspect of the story of the compassionate father most impacted you?

1. Read the story of the prodigal son in Luke 15:11-22. Fill out the chart below with every detail you can find from the story:

Signs of the Child's Rebellion	Signs of the Father's Compassion

2. What can you learn about the Father's response when it comes to

   —a situation in your life in which you feel you need to "return" to your Father?

   —a situation in your child's life in which you need to be more like your heavenly Father in your response?

3. Read James 1:5-8 and answer the following questions:

   Who can ask for wisdom (verse 5)?

   How are we told to ask for wisdom (verse 6)?

   To whom does God provide wisdom (verses 5-7)?

   In what two ways does God give His wisdom (verse 5)?

4. Regardless of where your child is spiritually right now, insert their name(s) in the blanks below and pray these Scriptures over their lives:

   Create in _____ a pure heart, O God, and renew a steadfast spirit within him/her (Psalm 51:10). Though You have made _____ see troubles, many and bitter, You will restore _____'s life again; from the depths of the earth you will again bring _____ up. You will increase _____'s honor and comfort _____ once again (Psalm 71:20-21). Thank You that Your Word says I am convinced that neither death nor life, neither angels nor demons, neither the present nor the future, nor any powers, neither height, nor depth, nor anything else in all creation, will be able to separate _____ from the love of God that is in Christ Jesus our Lord.

9

I Wish I Could Do More

Secret 9: Surrendering to God Your
Tendency to Rescue

Mary recalls some of her scariest days as a mom.

Her oldest daughter, Annie, was attending college far from home and struggling with feeling hopeless—to the point of having suicidal thoughts. This brought Mary to her knees in prayer.

"During her first semester in college, Annie spiraled downward into depression," Mary said. "She was in another state far from home, and it was frightening to hear her say the words 'I want to kill myself.' It still takes my breath away thinking of the anguish and helplessness I felt when she verbalized that to me."

Mary and her husband, Ken, offered to bring Annie back home immediately to continue her schooling at a university down the street. But Annie was adamant about not coming home. She wanted to stay in school and work through her situation.

So Annie's parents reached out to her school for support and to several close friends for prayer, and remained in close contact with their daughter daily.

"Ken and I were able to get some professional counsel about how to handle this situation," Mary said. As they trusted God to minister to their daughter's heart thousands of miles away, He came through.

"It was a difficult year, but God brought Annie out of the depression and made her stronger. She excelled in her second, third, and fourth years of college. Cleary, Annie's first year away was a time of stretching for all of us. We look back with thankfulness."

Our Tendency to Rescue

There's nothing more debilitating for a mom than feeling like she can do nothing when her children are experiencing pain. Many moms I surveyed as I was writing this book told me that they longed for the assurance that their children would never have to suffer in any way. Yet as you've seen in previous chapters, God will often allow certain uncomfortable or "why this?" situations in our children's lives so He can build their character and their dependence on Him. Through their suffering, they come to know God in a deeper way—as their Rescuer, their Hero, their Deliverer, and The One Who Makes All Things Right.

How many a mom has felt helpless and wished she could do more as a child was...

- writhing in physical pain
- silently dealing with emotional pain
- struggling with an addiction
- missing home and she couldn't get to them
- being unfairly treated at school or on their job
- sick and she couldn't make them better

We are hardwired as moms to rush in and rescue. We want to swoop in, grab our kids, tuck them safely under our mother hen wings, and fly them off to a place of peace and comfort. But there comes a time, sometimes even when they're still small, that God wants to be the Mother Hen. He wants to be the Father-Protector, the Deliverer, the Hero. Yes, there's a reason God lets our kids go through situations in which we can't help. He wants to teach our children something about Himself that we can't do on our own just by *telling* them about God. He wants our kids to *experience Him* for themselves. And I can't help but feel there's an equally important reason He allows *us* to feel helpless as parents. God wants to teach *us* a few things about Himself too. He wants us convinced that, hands down, He can defend, protect, and care for our children far better than we can.

As Mom Stands By

My friend Chery told me it was a difficult time of "standing by"—but a precious time of having to trust God—when her son, Dustyn, landed his first job:

"Dustyn, at 19 years old, had applied for a part-time position in a store's department that was well-suited for him as he is hyperactive and very social. This position was physical with many different tasks. He ended up being assigned to another department full-time. I was immediately stressed as he knew nothing about the new department to which he had been assigned. But he was confident and said, 'They say they'll teach me everything I need to know. Besides, Mom, God is in control.'

"*Yes, indeed He is,* I thought.

"Dustyn began his job with an interim boss while his regular boss was on vacation. Everything went well for the first week and a half. Then his regular boss came back and she was *horrible*. She was harsh and verbally abusive toward him; he could do nothing right. She threatened his job constantly, and when she wasn't happy with his work, she would make him clock out and come back to finish, sometimes for up to two hours longer. I encouraged him to see the store manager and discuss his work environment or file a complaint with the union. But his boss had convinced him that she was tight with the store manager, and he felt if he made any trouble, it would certainly cost him his job. He just wanted to take everything to God.

"So we prayed and prayed...and prayed some more (mostly for a kind, gentle, boss and work environment, God's protection, and the courage to work in the face of challenge). When I would pick him up after work he was very emotional, and he would be emotional when I dropped him off. He knew he would be 'beaten up' all day and didn't want to go. Before and after work, we would sit in the car and pray together. He would say, 'Mom, I know I'm having this experience for a reason and that God is in control. He is working on me, but it is so hard.' Our son would say that frequently so I knew he was trusting God and moving forward. It was a good lesson for me as I continued to cover him in prayer.

"As Dustyn's mom, I had *very* un-Christian thoughts about this woman who was harassing him and I had to do a lot of praying over that as well. During the three-month probationary period of Dustyn's job, he got to know everyone in the store and developed many nice friendships with co-workers. At the end of his probation, his boss gave him a bad review and he was moved to the original position he had applied for, which was a demotion. He told me he was going to say good-bye to his boss and thank her for all she had taught him. I was stunned, and he said, 'God would want that.' (That was another good lesson for me.) When Dustyn did say good-bye, his boss said, 'Too bad that you couldn't cut it here.'

"My face went into the 'just let me at her' look. My son reached out and took my shoulders and said, 'Mom, we need to pray for her if anything. She must have experienced something pretty bad to be so mean.' There it was—another good lesson for my mother's heart.

"It's been a year now that Dustyn has been on the job. He has excelled in his position and he is frequently requested by managers and cashiers for certain needs. He has a wonderful customer base and great co-worker relationships. When he sees his old boss, he says, 'She throws it at me, I throw it right back, and we have a laugh.'

"God grew us through this experience more than words can say. God taught me so much about trusting in Him—to not step in and rescue our son, but to turn to God and let our son make his way in difficulty through prayer and trusting Him. Though I couldn't have ever imagined it at the time, I feel grateful for the experience. I feel peace."

Chery said she was able to experience peace once she practiced Psalm 46:10: "Be still, and know that I am God."

Don't Rush In

It's difficult to be still when our kids are being harassed, treated unfairly, or bullied. But as much as you want to rescue and defend and save your children, resist the urge. The older they get, the more God wants them to start relying on *Him* to do the rescuing. So, let Him do what only He can do in a far better way than you can.

Here are some reasons you should resist the urge to rush in and, instead, let God work it out:

God Always Has a Better Plan

Rushing in to rescue your child could actually interfere with a far better plan that God is working out. He often has a better rescue in mind, and a lesson for you to learn in the meantime.

Judy knows this from experience. She was frustrated that she couldn't help her son, Jason, who was choosing to honor God and appeared to be penalized for it in his job situation. Yet that's exactly where God wanted Judy so that *He* could show Jason that He is a God worth depending on.

Jason, who was just out of high school, was given the opportunity to play guitar with the worship band at his church. It wasn't something just anyone was allowed to do, and he took the position and privilege seriously. In addition to weekly Bible study and accountability among the other band members, Jason had to be available on certain weekends to play for the Saturday evening and Sunday morning services. So in order to fulfill his obligations to this unpaid position, he asked the boss at his paying job for certain weekends off.

Jason's boss soon began making it difficult for him to take weekends off when he needed to play guitar at church. So Jason graciously quit his job and got another job somewhere else that allowed him weekend availability.

"In the meantime, a different boss at his former job who was higher up asked Jason, 'What will it take for you to come back?' Jason explained his situation about needing certain weekends off and said he couldn't come back, and thanked him anyway. Not only was Jason hired back to that original job with *every* weekend off, but also in a *higher* position with *more* pay.

"God sure blessed Jason for sticking to his commitment to put God first!" Judy said. And looking back now, she realizes there was never a cause for worry, or a need to rescue. God worked everything out even better than she or her son could have expected.

God Wants to Help Our Children Resolve It Themselves

At the beginning of this chapter, I shared about Annie's struggle with depression and suicidal thoughts. Today she is happily married and awaiting an assignment with her husband in the Peace Corps. Most exciting of all, Annie now has opportunities to talk with other girls who are feeling hopeless and battling suicidal thoughts. Annie's past experiences—and her learning how to depend on God through them—make it possible for her to minister to others who face similar struggles. That appears to be a pattern in this book, doesn't it? God took an area of a child's life that had a mom worried and used it to develop the character of that child and, in some cases, even give that child a ministry to others.

Sometimes God wants to help our children resolve a situation themselves so He can make this scripture come true in their lives:

> Praise be to the God and Father of our Lord Jesus Christ, the Father of compassion and the God of all comfort, *who comforts us in all our troubles, so that we can comfort those in any trouble with the comfort we ourselves receive from God...* (2 Corinthians 1:3-4).

Can you see now that if Mary had flown in (literally) to rescue her daughter and bring her home from college that Annie might not have gained the trust and experience that enables her to now help other young girls?

God Wants Our Children to Ask Him for Help

Sometimes, in our attempts to rescue, we advise our children to compromise or do what's safe but not necessarily God-honoring. We say things like:

"You better not ask for Sundays off because you might lose your job."

"You better do what your teacher says, even if it's against your personal beliefs. You wouldn't want to sacrifice your grade."

"You better not ask for that. You don't want to look like you're being lazy or selfish."

But isn't God bigger than our situations in which we think we need to compromise? If He can rescue three Israelite teens out of a fiery furnace for refusing to bow down to a false god (Daniel 3); and if He could rescue one young man from the mouths of hungry lions when he, too, refused to bow down to a fake god (Daniel 6); then He can certainly help our children out of much lesser dilemmas when they act on their convictions.

My daughter learned this recently when she went to work for the Walt Disney Company at California Adventure Park. It was a dream-come-true job for her. And yet, in her heart of hearts, she wanted to be able to continue to attend and be involved in a church with her family.

The company's motto is "We work so the world can play," and therefore employees (Disney calls them "cast members") are expected to work every weekend and holiday—the resort's busiest times.

Dana's heart was to keep this job and yet have Sunday mornings off. She also really wanted to spend Easter Sunday, Thanksgiving Day, Christmas Eve, and Christmas Day with her family. Mother's Day and Father's Day would be nice too, she thought, but since they fall on Sundays, she probably shouldn't get her hopes up. Yet, we prayed about it. As every holiday approached, my husband and I asked God to put His favor on her when it came to her supervisors and to allow her to be home or in church on the days that were important for her to do so. And so, she began her job asking for Sunday mornings off.

Dana, who was newly hired and didn't have any seniority with the company, has since received *every Sunday morning* (and sometimes the entire day) off of work. She has also proceeded to ask for every major holiday as it approached on the calendar. And to this day, she has received every holiday and day off that she has requested. *Every single one.*

Jesus told His followers, "Ask and it will be given to you; seek and you will find; knock and the door will be opened to you. For everyone who asks receives; the one who seeks finds; and to the one who knocks, the door will be opened" (Matthew 7:7-8).

God is pleased by our requests that require Him to go to bat for us. And when we, as moms, are not rushing in to rescue, that leaves our children with no other alternative than to go to God with their requests and wait on Him for their rescue. It's a powerful lesson for them, early on, that God can come to their aid. It develops their faith. And it helps them become people of prayer.

Knowing When to Back Off

There are times when it's hard for us as moms to see a child in a tough situation. And yet if we attempt to intercede, we only end up interfering rather than backing off and letting God work. We want to be there for our children, but sometimes it's hard to let go. Listen to the following words of wisdom from moms who had to learn that sometimes it's best to back off.

Let Them Grow Up

Nancy, who in chapter 5 had to trust God with her teenage daughter when she was starting to hang out with the wrong crowd, realized recently that it's finally time to let her now 20-year-old grow up and take responsibility for herself.

"Even though my daughter is older I am still concerned that she walk the right path (going to church, reading the Bible, getting to know God), be a responsible adult (paying bills on time, getting enough healthy food in her diet, getting places safely) and make the right choices. I learned a few years ago that after I did everything I could to give my daughter the tools she needed to live like God wants her to live, I had to back off and trust God. I need to make sure I'm not trying to control her, but rather, simply love her and be there for her."

Let Them Remember What They've Been Taught

One mom, whose daughter is now in her thirties, shared this:

"When my daughter left for college more than 400 miles away, it was her first time so far away alone, with no family near at all.

Adjusting was hard, but the Lord kept impressing upon my heart, *Trust your teaching; trust your teaching.* My prayers then changed concerning my daughter. Instead of prayers only for protection and godly friends, I said, 'Please bring all things to her remembrance at the times it will be most needed.'"

If we are constantly present and telling our kids what to do, when will they learn to practice common sense, exercise good judgment, and display discernment? Let them call to mind all they've been taught. It will do them good.

Let Them Fail and Learn from It

Darlene, who has raised three sons, says this about letting go and letting our children fail:

"Everyone thinks that when your children are young that it is the most difficult time. Yet the teenage years and beyond are actually harder to endure. Your children are on their own, making decisions and choices for themselves—choices that can affect their whole life. A mother wonders, *Did I train them right and will they follow what I taught them?* I think the most difficult area, for me, was to let my sons fail, to let God take care of them, and to realize that I am not God and I cannot fix everything.

"I found it easier to let go of my two older sons and entrust them to God, but for some reason I haven't done so well with my youngest. My youngest has been the most difficult and challenging. I or someone else was always fixing his problems and making life easier for him. Letting go and allowing him to hit rock bottom was the most difficult thing to do, and it's a journey I am still on.

"It is difficult for me to discern the difference between helping and enabling. You spend your time as a mother caring for the needs of your children, then they are grown, and you start letting them attain their own goals. With my youngest, I got stuck. I forgot to quit helping. He kept getting into financial difficulty, and I would rescue him. I felt I was the only person who could take care of the situation.

"Then one day God laid a message on my heart that I was not God, nor did my son need my help. Turning my youngest son loose and asking God to do what was needed in his life was the most difficult decision I have ever made. I still have to keep praying that God will prevent me from rescuing my son. I know that God loves my son more than I do, and that He knows what my son needs."

I can identify with Darlene's inner conflict, can't you? We love our children and want to be their rescuer. But sometimes the best thing we can do—in addition to prayer—is to let them hit bottom so God can pull them out. We need to pray for discernment so we know when to step back, or when to (with God's direction) initiate a rescue.

When It's Time to Act

I don't want to close this chapter by implying that all you need to do is pray about a situation when there is, in fact, something that you as a mom can do.

If our child truly needs help, and we sense God telling us to do more than just pray, that's when we need to act.

Brenda experienced this recently when her daughter, Hannah, graduated from college a semester early and decided to be a nanny in Italy for three months. Hannah was 21 and well-travelled, having been to London with friends, Europe with her family, and Nepal and India with her father when she was 13. This, however, was the first time she had flown to another country alone. And she would be staying with people she didn't know.

As soon as Hannah arrived, she found the situation very unlike what she had been told.

"I got there and didn't like it at all," Hannah said. "I couldn't sleep. Plus, I was alone in a home way out in the country, too far to go into town on my own. The kids were obnoxious and undisciplined. It was a stressful situation. After a few days I thought *I don't know if this is going to get better.*"

One day Hannah was feeling stressed and in tears, she called her mother. "I was in complete hysterics," Hannah said.

"But it was a silent cry," Brenda added. "She was crying hard, but she kept it inside. She was having a panic attack. I'd never seen her that way before."

A few minutes after the call, during which Brenda tried to calm her daughter down, she realized Hannah's anxiety was out of character for someone so independent. She sensed in her spirit something wasn't right. Brenda texted her daughter and asked, "Do you want me to come there?" She half-expected Hannah to say, "No, Mom. I'll be fine. I'll work this out." Instead, Hannah gave a resounding "Yes!"

By 11:00 the next morning, Brenda was on a plane to Italy. And upon hearing her mom was coming, Hannah slept four hours. It was the first time she'd slept that long during the six days she had been there.

Upon arrival, Brenda discovered the ill and oppressive conditions Hannah was enduring. What's more, she was locked inside the house all day because the doors locked from the inside and she hadn't been given a key. So she told her daughter, "We are leaving."

Brenda said, "I went to help her get adjusted. I never imagined I'd be bringing her back home with me."

Hannah said, "I'm so glad my mom came. I needed her to validate my situation and see that I wasn't being crazy. I wouldn't have been able to just leave and feel okay about it without my mom seeing the situation for herself. I probably would've stayed and been miserable and stuck it out if my mom hadn't come."

Hannah said her mother's help in getting her out of that emotionally unhealthy situation is something for which she will always be grateful.

"Other parents probably would've said to their kids 'You paid for a flight, you made a commitment, you owe something to this person, so you need to stick it out.' But my mom helped me get perspective," Hannah said. "She told me, 'You're an adult. You're miserable. You didn't know you were getting into this situation because you were misled in many ways, and you don't owe these people anything. For your health and well-being, you need to leave.'

"She rescued me from a bad situation. I knew I could always rely on her, and this was the biggest thing I've ever needed her for."

Be Strong, but Soft

There will be times when your child needs to know that you will go to bat for him or her, regardless of the cost. (And it was quite an expensive trip for Brenda to take on at the last minute.) Brenda said, "I'm of the belief that sometimes we all just need a soft place to land. We learned from it. I didn't say 'I hope you learned your lesson' or lecture Hannah about it."

You and I need to pray for discernment to know when to back off, and when to make ourselves available.

A Plan to Replace Worry

For all the times that you *won't* be able to rescue your child, you will need a plan that will help you to replace worry and anxiety with God's peace. Here are some practical ways to do that:

1. Replace Your Fear with God's Truth

When Annie struggled with suicidal thoughts, Mary realized she needed to replace her fears with God's truth.

"Breaking the cycle of fearful thinking and replacing it with God's truth is a daily discipline of prayer," she said.

We fear that our child is on his or her own, but the truth is that God has said, "Never will I leave you; nor will I ever forsake you" (Hebrews 13:5). That goes for you, as well as your child.

We fear that the worst possible scenario might happen to our child, but God says, "I know the plans I have for you...plans to prosper you and not to harm you, plans to give you hope and a future" (Jeremiah 29:11). And that goes for your child as well.

2. Rely on God's Promises

Once we know the truth of God's Word, we can rely on it during times of uncertainty, or times when we feel we should be doing something but can't. At the close of this chapter I have listed some Scripture passages that moms have relied upon when they weren't able to rescue their child. You can claim those verses and meditate on them as well.

3. Rally with Other Moms in Prayer

Mary said, "Being a part of a mom's prayer group strengthened me from the inside out and connected me with other moms whom I have grown to know, love, and appreciate. I was encouraged by their powerful prayers for my daughters. It has also been a privilege for me to get to know their children through prayer and celebrate answered prayers together over the years." (In chapter 1 I listed some moms groups and opportunities to connect with moms. Or, you can find another mom and ask if the two of you can commit to praying together weekly for your children.)

God's Got This

God's got your child's situation under control, whether you believe it or not. Whether you acknowledge it or not. Whether you act or not. So doesn't it make sense to trust the One who can work out the details of your child's life much better than you can?

Judy is now convinced of that because of how God worked in Jason's life. Dana, Hugh, and I are convinced of that because of how God has worked in Dana's job situation. Mary and Ken have seen God do incredible things in Annie's life. And you can be convinced of His ability to rescue as well. It all starts with asking. And then comes the time to trust Him.

Putting It into Practice
Surrendering Your Tendency to Rescue

Here are some verses you can start praying right now in lieu of being able to rescue your child from a present or future situation. These verses will give you the peace you need in the times when you can't help:

> Lord, You say you will fight for _____; I
> need only to be still (Exodus 14:14). Fight for _____
> in the situations in which You know he/she needs You.
> Be _____'s rock of refuge, to which he/she can
> always go; give the command to save _____, for
> you are his/her rock and fortress. Deliver _____,
> O my God, from the hand of the wicked, from the grasp
> of evil and cruel men (Psalm 71:3-4). When _____
> passes through the waters, You will be with him/her; and
> when _____ passes through the rivers, they
> will not sweep over him/her. When _____

walks through the fire, he/she will not be burned; the flames will not set _____ ablaze (Isaiah 43:2). Thank You that Your Word says that no weapon forged against _____ will prevail. This is the heritage of the servants of the Lord, and this is their vindication (Isaiah 54:17). Finally, Your Word says _____ can do all things through Christ who strengthens him/her (Philippians 4:13). Strengthen _____ in Your name. Amen.

....

Becoming a Worry-Free Mom —in Community

....

For Thought or Discussion: Describe a time when you couldn't help your child with something, but God worked the situation out.

1. Which is the most challenging for you right now, and why?

   • Letting your children grow up

   • Letting them remember your teachings

   • Letting them fail and learn from their failure

2. What is one way you can practice each of the following steps in the plan to replace worry?

   • Replace your fear with God's truth

- Rely on God's promises

- Rally with other moms in prayer

3. In order to rely on God's promises, read each of the
   verses below and describe your "help" or comfort:

   Exodus 14:14—

   Psalm 121:1-3—

   Psalm 91:1-2—

   Psalm 18:6—

   Isaiah 12:2—

   Isaiah 40:29-31—

   Romans 8:31—

10

You Want to Do *What* with Your Life?

Secret 10: Trusting God with Their Future

One morning not too long ago I was praying—and trying not to worry—about my daughter's future.

I wrote this in my journal, as a way of dialoguing with God:

> It's now 30 days until Dana graduates from her internship with the Disney College program and has to move out of the college program housing. But because she will stay with the company, she needs to find housing in that area. Yet she hasn't been assured of full-time status and is uncertain what her take-home pay will be, so she's trying to determine what she can afford to pay for her rent and utilities.
>
> To add to that uncertainty, Dana is looking for housing in a part of the country where it is extremely expensive to live. So many variables. And so many prayers. It's like I want You to know all the options, God. But of course You already know Your plans for her.
>
> God, please give her favor with her supervisor so she is moved to full-time status so she can make enough money to live near her job. And please help her to find a safe, inexpensive place to live.

> Lord, can You please bring her a roommate, too, who can share living costs with her? And not just any roommate, but someone she knows and trusts? How about someone who knows and trusts You too?

> Lord, please help her to trust You and to pray to You about all of this, just as much as I am!

And then it occurred to me that when I was Dana's age, it was situations like this that built my trust in my Savior. It was situations like this—when things got right down to the wire—that taught me to pray and step out in faith, and see God come through for me just in the nick of time.

It was situations like this that helped me take ownership of my faith.

That is what I want for my daughter more than anything else. More than a satisfying career for her. More than a man of God to become her husband. More than her success and financial independence. What I want most is for her to grow in her faith and dependence on the Lord.

I'm sure that's what you want for your child or children too.

And situations that typically cause moms to worry are the kinds of situations that God often uses to grow His children—especially when it comes to their future.

So I will wait. I will pray. I will trust that God will grow her faith in Him while I am waiting and praying. And I will rest—as if He already has it worked out. Which, I'm sure, He has.

I prayed Jeremiah 29:11 for Dana that day, inserting her name in the passage:

> You know the plans You have for Dana, plans to prosper her and not to harm her, plans to give her hope and a future. Then Dana will call upon You and come and

pray to You and You will listen to her. She will seek You and find You when she seeks You with all her heart (see verses 12-13).

And then I got it.

God has my child in a place of uncertainty right now because of the work He wants to do in her life as well as mine. He wants *her* to depend on Him. He wants *her* to call on Him for help. He wants *her* to be on her knees, desperate for and waiting upon Him. Oh how wonderful it is that He wants her to experience all of that. I will not rob her of that joy by trying to work everything out for her. I will not cheat her from experiencing God for herself.

My prayer then became this:

> Lord, help me to quietly trust You as You work in my daughter's life. Help me to encourage her in her faith at the appropriate times and be her support when she needs it. And don't let me take Your place or interrupt what You want to do in her life.

After I prayed that, I was comforted to read these words in a devotional that same morning: "Have you been asking God what He is going to do? He will never tell you. God does not tell you what He is going to do—He reveals to you who He is."[25]

God's Revelation of Himself

Isn't that the primary reason we worry in the first place? We want to know *what* God is going to do and *when* and *how* He's going to do it. We want Him to show us the plan so we can give Him our opinion on it. We play out all the scenarios in our minds and we even give God ideas about what we think He should do. And all this time, God just wants to reveal to us who He is—the One who holds the future in His hands.

God wants me to be convinced that He will guide Dana to her hope and future. He wants to reveal to you that His plans for your child are far better than yours. He wants you and me to experience Him as the *God Who Always Comes Through.*

Our Hopes for Them

I'm sure you have high hopes for your children's future. You want them to far exceed what you've been able to accomplish in life. You've seen the gentle spirit in your son and hoped he will be a pastor, or you've seen your daughter's heart for children and hoped she will be a loved teacher or a content wife and mom.

As much as you think about what your children's futures might hold, especially career-wise, I want to challenge you to consider their futures in terms of their hearts. What they choose to do as a career is for this life only. It's for the here and now on Earth, and it may even change several times before they find what fits just right for them. Yet what they choose to do with their hearts is for eternity.

When we grasp that truth—that the desire and direction of their heart and their obedience to God is more important than anything else—we will be able to more easily trust God with their future.

I suppose the average mom, whether she is a follower of Christ or not, would say she wants her children to have "a good life."

But what is that, really? Comfort? Pleasure? Happiness? Monetary success? The ownership of a big house and lots of stuff? Those are shallow pursuits in the scope of eternity. I fear, after what I've seen most of my life, that a child who grows up too comfortable without challenges will be complacent or bored at best, spoiled and selfish at worst.

What if your greatest hope for your children was that they experience God in a life-changing way and then live their lives to serve God and others?

Welcome the Strain

Oswald Chambers said, "God does not give us overcoming life—He gives us life as we overcome. The strain of life is what builds our strength. If there is no strain, there will be no strength."[26]

Ironically, it's the *strain of life* we hope to help our children avoid. Yet it is the strain and struggles that build their character. As we learned in chapter 2, "unsafe" situations are often the ones that cause us and our children to more closely depend on Him. And as we saw in chapter 3, the "Why this?" struggles build their character and give them a testimony to others.

Can you welcome the strain or even the unsafe when it comes to your children's future, knowing that God has them right where He wants them to be?

Dawn's Surrender

My friend Dawn Marie shared with me her point of surrender when her son faced a life-and-death situation.

"My youngest son, an athlete, was in high school at the time. One day he collapsed in a doctor's office. My husband and I were worried that he had a serious heart problem that would lead to early death. It was scary waiting for the results of tests, but the Lord assured me that my son was safe in His arms until it was time for him to go home to heaven. I was able to relax in God's presence and faithful care."

That kind of rest comes only through a trust relationship with God—one that you have been cultivating and practicing. It's the kind of relationship in which you surrender to God's will regardless of how it might conflict with your plans for your children. It requires that you defer to His wisdom even if you don't understand it.

Dawn Marie now understands that, at the time, God was preparing her for a *lifetime* of having to trust her son to God's protection.

"My son had another scary situation as a young man, and the Lord gave me the same reassurance. And I think this was all a dress rehearsal for our situation today," she said. "My son is now in a high-risk job, and safety will *always* be an issue."

Darlene's Dilemma

God had to work on Darlene's heart too when her youngest son asked her, two years ago, to pray that he would be accepted into the military. Because he has a blood disease and has had his spleen removed, Darlene told him "there's no way you can join the military in that condition."

But it was her son's desire, one he felt God had given him.

"He told me 'Mom, I really believe God is calling me to join the military. Please pray for me.' I have never wanted my sons in the military, especially with all that is going on in the Middle East. I refused to pray for him to be in the military.

"But my middle son told me that it was better to be in a war zone in God's will than safe at home out of it. (I just hate it when things you taught your children come back to bite you.) So I prayed. And God answered. The military doesn't list his blood disorder as an illness or disease. My youngest son is now in the Army National Guard. I can't say I have perfect peace, but I know it was God's will. I'm still praying for him and for God to direct him. I know now that it will be okay, no matter what happens."

Having the awareness that God is engineering the circumstances of our children's lives helps us to trust Him with their futures.

Preparing Them for Life

As our children grow up, we need to listen to their hearts when they let us know their desires and inclinations for their future. And as God makes it clear where they are headed, we need to let them go, let them get hurt, and give them time.

Listen to Their Hearts

Angela, a mom of four children, remembers the day she and her husband had an opportunity to talk to three of their children about their future plans. And they came to realize that sometimes God plants the seed of His will in children's hearts while they're still young.

"One year we took the kids to the Houston Livestock Show and Rodeo," Angela said. "On the way home, I asked each of my children what they might want to be when they grew up.

"After letting them know that their daddy and I believed in them and knew that they could be anything God placed in their hearts to be, we asked each of them to take turns answering. Chelsie, our oldest, answered first and said she had decided to be an artist. Evidently she was influenced by the incredible artwork she had seen in the exhibit halls at the show.

"Levi, age three, busted out with 'I want to be a *bullrider*!' After catching my heart in my throat as any momma would do, I smiled and said, 'Oh, wow...that would be exciting!' while secretly hoping God might place another dream in his heart...one that might involve less contact with a raging wild animal!

"Next I turned to Bailey, ready for a more sensible answer. She said, 'I want to be a tennis player.'

"A *what*? I quickly tried to figure out what might have inspired this. We didn't play tennis; we didn't watch tennis on TV; we never even *talked* about tennis! So I asked her how she had arrived at the decision to become a tennis player. She sat up straight and, with a twinkle in her eye, declared, 'The outfits are just *so cute*!' We all rolled with laughter along with her, agreeing that tennis outfits were adorable and she would look amazing sporting the latest styles.

"And as I recall this special memory, my heart is full knowing she is about to embark on an amazing journey as an international fashion model who is stepping out on the verse that I have prayed over my kids their whole lives:

> You are the light of the world. A town built on a hill cannot be hidden. Neither do people light a lamp and put it under a bowl. Instead they put it on its stand, and it gives light to everyone in the house. In the same way, let your light shine before others, that they may see your good deeds and glorify your Father in heaven (Matthew 5:14-16).

Let Them Go

I applaud Angela's excitement about her daughter's "amazing journey as an international fashion model." Sometimes we fear our children entering secular professions or fields, thinking they will be much safer if they stay within the bounds of the "Christian world." But God never called us to a "Christian world." In fact, such a thing doesn't exist. He called us to be lights in the darkness, *wherever* we are. And if He is guiding your child toward a field that looks lost or dark or broken, it's quite possible that He knows your child will be a much-needed light in that darkness.

Letting our children go also means leaving them in God's hands—even physically and geographically.

Florence is a major in the Salvation Army and the mother of three grown children. *Three* children that she had to leave—each in a different state—when it came to moving the family as a result of new assignments. During those times when they packed up, moved on, and left a child behind, she learned firsthand that God is truly able to care for them even better than she could.

First they had to leave their oldest son in Alaska just after he graduated from high school. He wanted to stay there when Florence got transferred to Louisiana. Then after their daughter graduated from high school in Louisiana, they left her there and were stationed again in Alaska. Finally, they had to leave their youngest son in Oregon when they moved on to Santa Rosa, California.

"They survive, I need to be reminded," Florence said. "God is good indeed." Each of her children learned, as young adults, how to get by on their own without their parents close by. Florence said Joshua 1:9 has been a comfort to her with each separation from her children, and it remains a comfort to her today: "Have I not commanded you? Be strong and courageous. Do not be afraid; do not be discouraged, for the LORD your God will be with you wherever you go."

Florence knows that God will be with her children wherever *they* go too.

Let Them Hurt So They Will Grow

Finally, we have to let our children struggle so they will learn to depend on God for themselves.

Brenda, whose story you read in the previous chapter, says, "Even though you don't want your children to go through hard times, those times are necessary for building their character and faith. Even though it's hard to watch your children go through trials, they grow as a result. As I look back at the times that I grew the closest to God, it was during times of suffering."

Discerning Open Doors

As our children move away from home, they will inevitably experience open doors of opportunities. How will they know if an open door is from God, or just a distraction or detour from where they really want to be? Perhaps they already know for sure, and you are the one having a hard time understanding whether something is actually God's will. Here are some guidelines that will help you experience peace or equip you to instruct your child when it comes to determining whether God is the One who is opening the door to their opportunities:

1. The Door God Opens Will Never Contradict His Word

Your child may see opportunities to make more money as an open door from God, even though the opportunity means a compromise in some way (tending a bar when they have personal convictions against drinking, working on a Sunday when it will keep them from regular fellowship or service in their church, living far from their spouse when it might invite temptation, and so on). Yet God will not put an opportunity in front of His child that contradicts the clear instruction of His Word. If an open door requires compromise or bending Scripture to justify the opportunity, then it's likely that God is not the one opening that door. Anything that contradicts His Word is more likely a test or temptation.

2. The Door God Opens Will Be Accompanied by Confirmation

In Matthew 18:15-16, Jesus laid out instructions for confronting sin among believers: "If they will not listen, take one or two others along, so that 'every matter may be established by the testimony of two or three witnesses.'" I believe the same applies when it comes to God confirming something in His Word. He will often confirm or establish a matter by "two or three witnesses" whether they be verses from the Bible, advice from a pastor or well-respected person who is grounded in Scripture, or circumstances. Through prayer, seeking godly counsel, and careful evaluation of circumstances, your child should be able to tell whether that open door (and its confirmations) are truly coming from God.

3. The Door God Opens Will Require You to Depend on Him

God is not going to give us something that will alienate us from Him or make us believe we no longer need Him. He is a God of relationship, and a God who insists upon being first in our lives. Therefore, if your child says, "I can't do this unless God goes before me," or "I can do this, but only with God's help and leading," it is probably something God is calling them to do.

Hebrews 11:6 says: "And without faith it is impossible to please *Him*, for he who comes to God must believe that He is and *that* He is a rewarder of those who seek Him" (NASB). Many times an open door from God is one that allows our faith to be stretched and strengthened. That, after all, is God's objective for His children: to have them grow in faith and Christlikeness.

Giving Them a Confident Future

As your children walk the path toward their future, make sure you're not a mom who holds on too tight, worries about them, or makes them feel guilty about leaving you. Here are some ways you can help them walk that path with confidence:

1. Build Your Own Life—Brenda, who helped her daughter Hannah get out of a bad situation in Italy (see chapter 9), said that some moms spend their lives obsessing over their children and having to be there for everything.

"If you are one who *needs* your children around, start doing things to grow your own confidence so you can be an example to them of how to be confident and find their way. A lot of moms put their kids in sports, piano lessons, dance, and so on to build their child's confidence, but they should be modeling that confidence to their kids as well."

Brenda's daughter, Hannah, said, "A lot of moms are dependent on their children for companionship and purpose. Then when their kids move out, they feel they don't have anyone and their life lacks purpose. They can become obsessed with trying to hold onto their kids."

2. Be Their Example—Cheryl, who has raised six children into responsible adults, advises: "Step back as a mom and think about what you want your kids to be. Then live it out. I was determined not to be a selfish mom, so I sought God in how to live my life for Him, not for me. I spent time in God's Word regularly so I could be still and know that God was God and I was not. When I felt the Spirit prompting me to help another person, I did so—whether it was caring for someone's kids, bringing a meal, or praying for someone. It was not always convenient or easy, but I was enabled by God's grace. My kids remember me making meals for others, leading a small group, helping in the church nursery, and loaning a vehicle regularly to a lower-income family who needed a car to run errands. Today I am blessed to hear how my kids are carrying on the torch of service not because I preached it, but because I modeled it.

"It was also important for me to model to my kids what I expected from them. I had to admit when I was wrong, confess my errors to them, and ask for their forgiveness."

3. Be Strong for Them—Finally, we need to be moms who don't fall apart, worry ourselves sick, or become someone our children end up worrying about because of how we are handling—or unable to handle—*their* situations. Be strong so your children will keep sharing with you how you can pray for them. We want our children, all their lives, to be calling home and saying, "Pray for me," not telling someone else "Don't tell my mom. She won't be able to handle it."

Releasing Them into God's Hands

Our job, as godly parents, is to help our children become less dependent on us and more dependent on God. And for our children to learn that, we must release them.

Brenda shared with me how she was finally able to let her children go in order to build her own life:

"The biggest growing time for me as a parent was when my kids went off to college. I realized they were God's, but when they left home for college, I had to *really* give them to God. I went through a long difficult process of giving up control of them. It was a process of surrender."

How exactly did she do that?

"We hold onto things with tight fists," she said. "For me, surrender involved opening up my fists and saying 'They are Yours, God.'

"I never had control, but I *thought* I did. It was a physical, verbal surrendering to God—'You are in control and I can't do this anymore. I release them to You, even though it's hard for me to do so. I ask You to take them and keep them.'"

Just as surrender to Christ is something we do daily, surrendering our kids to the Lord is something we are to do daily as well.

Now when Brenda's children discuss their futures with her, like her son's recent decision to go overseas and work in a ministry, this is the process she goes through:

"I talk to God about it. I think it through. I ask my children questions to find out more. And then I talk to God some more. It's always a process—a conversation with God in which He begins to give me peace as I turn situations over to Him. I pray that God will give my children mentors in their new situations and that He will open their eyes to things I wouldn't be able to.

"Finally," Brenda says, "I have to remember that I have surrendered these kids to God. They are His. And if God calls my kids to do something that I think is dangerous, who am I to argue? If He's calling them, He will care for them."

A Lifestyle of Trust

My heart is heavy as I close out this book, especially this chapter on trusting God with our children's futures. In what I believe is not a coincidence, I learned just the other day that my high school friend and his wife lost their 16-year-old daughter in a tragic car accident. She was driving home from volleyball practice and apparently overcorrected the steering wheel when her car started to go off the road. Her car was sideswiped by a semi. She was airlifted to a regional medical center, where she died several hours later.

This young lady had been very involved in her youth group and was considered a model student by her teachers, coaches, and peers. And she was called home long before what anyone considered was her time.

How does a parent deal with something like that? If a child ends up getting cancer and dies slowly, there is opportunity for the family to say a gradual good-bye and experience closure. Yet in this case, a daughter who was so full of life and energy and promise one moment was gone the next.

There are no patterns or formulas to guarantee that our children will be spared of any suffering, or worse yet, an early death. There are no promises in Scripture that if we do all that we are called to do as parents (which I'm certain my friends did), that we will see our children live to a ripe old age and enjoy their children and grandchildren. There is only the deep assurance in our hearts that God knows what He's doing, that He is truly good, and that He numbered our children's days before there were any. God is the One who takes our kids home the exact moment He had decided—long before He gave them to us.

For many of us, it takes our whole lives to leave a lasting impact on this Earth. In this young girl's case, it took only a few short years. And through her passing and her memorial, she left the legacy of a high school girl who loved the Lord, lived to the fullest, and glorified Him even in her death.

In the scope of eternity, which God alone sees, some of us make a greater impact on this Earth in much less time. Who are we to question the Creator as to His purpose and timeline for each thing He has created? If He creates a beautiful rose to bloom only a short time and never to be seen again, that is certainly His prerogative.

As I contemplated this, I was comforted by these words from A.W. Tozer:

> To the child of God, there is no such thing as accident. He travels an appointed way. The path he treads was chosen for him when as yet he was not, when as yet he had existence only in the mind of God.
>
> Accidents may indeed appear to befall him and misfortune stalk his way; but these evils will be so in appearance only and will seem evil only because we cannot read the secret script of God's hidden providence and so cannot discover the ends at which He aims...
>
> The man of true faith may live in the absolute assurance that his steps are ordered by the Lord. For him, misfortune is outside the bounds of possibility. He cannot be torn from this earth one hour ahead of the time which God has appointed, and he cannot be detained on earth one moment after God is done with him here. He is not a waif of the wide world, a foundling of time and space,

but a saint of the Lord and the darling of His particular care.[27]

You and I—and our children—are *darlings* of His particular care. And so, while my heart is saddened by what I can't even imagine my friends are experiencing today, there is hope in the goodness and the lovingkindness of God—that even though we don't know what He's doing, we know He can be trusted.

I am reassured, once again, that nothing ever takes God by surprise. And that no moment of our lives with our children is a wasted moment when we dedicate each and every one of them to the Lord by saying,

> God, this day is Yours. My life is Yours. And my child is Yours. Be God in their situation and mine. Lead us down the path *You* have for us and let us not complain if we don't understand it. There is no better place to be than in the palms of Your very capable hands.

Can you pray that prayer? As you do, you will find that God replaces your worry with His peace as He partners lovingly with you in the days ahead.

Putting It into Practice

....

A Prayer for My Child's Future

Once again, insert your child's name in the blanks and pray this for his or her future.

> Lord God, You have numbered _____'s days before any of them came to be. Help me to trust Your wisdom in how You have ordained those days (Psalm 139:16). Please put it in _____'s heart to seek You with all his/her heart; do not let _____ stray from your commands (Psalm 119:10). May _____ trust in You with all his/her heart and lean not on his/her own understanding. In all _____'s ways, may he/she submit to You so You will make _____'s paths straight (Proverbs 3:5-6). Lord, may You give _____ the desire of his/her heart and make all his/her plans succeed (Psalm 20:4).
>
> Finally, help _____ to never be lacking in zeal but keep his/her spiritual fervor, serving You (Romans 12:11). I pray that _____ may live a life worthy of You and may please You in every way, bearing fruit in every good work, growing in the knowledge of You, being strengthened with all power according to Your glorious might (Colossians 1:9-11).

Becoming a Worry-Free Mom
—in Community

For Thought or Discussion: What is your greatest desire for your children's future?

1. Which of the three steps on pages 205-06 do you need to work on most so you don't worry about your children's future?

   • Build your life

   • Be their example

   • Be strong for them

2. What step(s) will you take this week to begin working on that area above?

3. How do the following verses encourage you to trust God with your child's future?

   Psalm 20:4—

   Psalm 37:4-5—

   Psalm 37:23-24—

   Proverbs 16:3—

   Jeremiah 29:11—

Philippians 1:6—

1 John 5:14-15—

4. If you don't already have a "life verse" for each of your children, this is a great time to pick one and begin praying it now. Choose from the verses above or look through previous chapters (and the prayers at the end of each chapter). Find a verse that is particularly applicable and meaningful for each of your children. Record their names below and their life verses.

Child(ren)'s Name(s):	Life Verse:

Appendix A

Drawing Nearer to the Perfect Parent

To partner with God—the Perfect Parent—we must first be His child, and He must be our heavenly Father. Although we are all God's creation, we are not all God's *children*. Scripture says each of us is a sinner from the time we are born (Psalm 51:5) and we are all, naturally, children of Satan, "the father of lies" (John 8:44). But God found a way to adopt us and make us His own (Romans 8:14-17).

To be cleansed of your sin and receive salvation in Christ (and therefore be considered God's child), you must surrender your heart to Him:

1. Admit you are a sinner by nature and there is nothing you can do on your own to make up for that sin in the eyes of a holy God (Romans 3:23).

2. Accept the sacrifice that God provided—the death of His righteous and sinless Son, Jesus, on the cross on your behalf—in order to bring you into communion with Him.

3. Enter into a love relationship with God, through Jesus, as a response to His love and forgiveness toward

you. (For more on developing and maintaining an intimate relationship with God, see my book, *Letting God Meet Your Emotional Needs*, available at www .StrengthForTheSoul.com.)

4. Surrender to God your right to yourself and acknowledge His right to carry out His plans for you and to mold you, shape you, and transform you for His pleasure.

5. Find a pastor or women's ministry director at a Bible-teaching church in your area or a trusted Christian friend and tell him or her of your decision to surrender your life to Christ. They will want to pray for you and get you the support and resources you need to grow in your new relationship with Jesus.

Daily Guide to Praying for Your Child

··

Scripture tells us we can experience peace, not anxiety, when we pray about what concerns us rather than worry (Philippians 4:6-7). Scripture also provides an excellent guide map for praying God's will for yourself and your children. In addition to praying regularly the prayers at the end of each chapter, here are some prayers you can lift up daily for your children. Insert your children's names in the blanks below, and pray for them according to the day of the week:

Monday: Pray for Their Safety and Protection

Thank You, Lord, that You are _____'s strength and shield (Psalm 84:11). You are _____'s hiding place; You will protect _____ from trouble and surround _____ with songs of deliverance (Psalm 32:7). I trust You that in peace _____ will lie down and sleep, for You alone, Lord, make _____ dwell in safety (Psalm 4:8). Help me to remember that when _____ passes through the waters, You will be with _____; and when _____ passes through the rivers, they will not sweep over _____. When _____ walks through the fire, _____ will not be burned; the flames will not set _____ ablaze (Isaiah 43:2).

Tuesday: Pray for Their Constant Awareness of God's Presence During Their Struggles

Where can _____ go from your Spirit? Where can _____ flee from Your presence? If _____ goes up to the heavens, You are there; if _____ makes (his/her) bed in the depths, You are there. If _____ rises on the wings of the dawn, if _____ settles on the far side of the sea, even there Your hand will guide _____, Your right hand will hold _____ fast (Psalm 139:7-10). Secure that knowledge in _____'s heart and mind, O God. May _____ not fear, but know that You are with him/her. May _____ not be dismayed, for You are God. You will strengthen _____ and uphold _____ with Your righteous right hand (Isaiah 41:10). You, God, are _____'s refuge and strength, an ever-present help in trouble. Therefore _____ will not fear, though the earth give way and the mountains fall into the heart of the sea, though its waters roar and foam and the mountains quake with their surging (Psalm 46:1-30). Help _____ to always know that if You are for him/her, no one can be against him/her (Romans 8:31).

Wednesday: Pray for Their Wisdom in Relationships

God, grant _____ the ability to be cautious in friendship, trusting only those whose hearts are pure (Proverbs 12:26). May _____ stay away from those with a perverse heart who stir up dissension and those who gossip and separate close friends (Proverbs 16:28). May _____ be a true friend who loves at all times (Proverbs 17:17) and realize it is more important to have a few close friends than to be the friend of many (Proverbs 18:24). May _____'s relationships always be pleasing to You. And please give _____ the wisdom, discernment, and strength to never be bound together with one who does not honor You, whether it be in a close friendship, a business partnership, or a dating relationship (2 Corinthians 6:14).

Thursday: Pray for Their Struggles and Temptations

God, may You turn _____'s eyes away from worthless things; preserve _____'s life according to Your Word (Psalm 119:34-37). If sinful people try to entice _____, don't let _____ give in to them (Proverbs 1:10). May _____ remember that no temptation has overtaken him/her but such as is common to man; and You are faithful and will not allow _____ to be tempted beyond what _____ is able to handle, but with the temptation will provide a way of escape so that _____ will be able to endure it (1 Corinthians 10:13). Above all else, guard _____'s heart, for it is the wellspring of life (Proverbs 4:23).

Friday: Pray for Their Maturity Growth

Lord, may _____, like Jesus, grow in wisdom, and in stature, and in favor with God and men (Luke 2:52). I pray that _____ may live a life worthy of You and may please You in every way; bearing fruit in every good work, growing in the knowledge of You, and being strengthened with all power according to Your glorious might (Colossians 1:9-11). May _____ realize daily that You are the One who causes *all* things—even the bad things—to work together for good to those who love You and are called according to Your purpose (Romans 8:28). May _____ realize too that You can work those things for _____'s eternal good to make _____ more like Your Son (Romans 8:29).

Saturday: Pray for Their Future

God, I praise You that You know the plans You have for _____, plans to not harm _____ but to give _____ a hope and a future (Jeremiah 29:11). May _____ trust in You with all his/her heart and lean not on his/her own understanding. In all _____'s ways, may he/she submit to You so You will make _____'s paths straight (Proverbs 3:5-6). May _____ commit to You whatever he/she does so _____'s plans will succeed (Proverbs 16:3). Lord, may You give _____ the desires of his/her heart and make all his/her plans succeed (Psalm 20:4).

Sunday: Pray for Their Spiritual Life

Lord, thank You that You began a good work in _____ and will carry it on to completion until the day of Christ Jesus (Philippians 1:6). Please put it in _____'s heart to seek You with all his/her heart; do not let _____ stray from Your commands (Psalm 119:10). Make _____'s ears attentive to wisdom, incline _____'s heart to understanding (Proverbs 2:2). Create in _____ a clean heart, O God, and renew a steadfast spirit within _____. Restore to _____ the joy of Your salvation and sustain _____ with a willing spirit (Psalm 51:10,12). I am convinced that nothing can ever separate _____ from Your love. Thank You that neither death nor life, angels nor demons, fears for today nor worries about tomorrow, and not even the powers of hell can separate _____ from Your love. No power in the sky above or in the earth below—indeed, nothing in all creation—will ever be able to separate _____ from Your love, which is revealed in Christ Jesus our Lord (Romans 8:38-39 NLT).

Notes

1. This information from Barna Research can be accessed at https://www.barna.org/barna-update/family-kids/669-tired-stressed-but-satisfied-moms-juggle-kids-career-identity#.U78DELGgrZJ.

2. This is a description of the "Wonder Women FRAMES" called "Navigating the Challenges of Motherhood, Career, and Identity" by Kate Harris. This product, offered by Barna Research Online, can be accessed at www.barna.org and then searching the terms "Wonder Women." See https://www.barna.org/component/virtuemart/books/wonder-women-detail?Itemid=0.

3. Stephanie Shott, *The Making of a Mom* (Grand Rapids: Revell, 2014), p. 12.

4. Numbers 12:3.

5. Robert Jeffress, *I Want More!* (Colorado Springs: Waterbrook, 2003), pp. 106-7.

6. Jeffress, p. 107.

7. For more on The Mom Initiative, see www.themominitiative.com or email Stephanie Shott at stephanie@themominitiative.com. You can also find them on Facebook at www.facebook.com/TheMOMInitiative and Twitter: @themominitiative.

8. For more informaton on SMORE, see www.smoreforwomen.org or contact Gail Showalter at singelmoms@smoreforwomen.org. Her blog can be found at smoreforwomen.wordpress.com.

9. Oswald Chambers, *My Utmost for His Highest*, ed. James Reimann (Grand Rapids: Discovery House, 1992), February 7.

10. According to the American SIDS Institute, the rate of SIDS has fallen more than 50 percent since 1983, down to 2500 cases per year in the United States. That number reflects only a tiny fraction of infants born in the US. And according to the National Center for Missing and Exploited Children, there were only five infant abductions (by individuals who were not parents or guardians) out of more than four million births in 2008, and all five were recovered unharmed. So the chances of your baby or child being kidnapped are extremely small (source: http://www.justmommies.com/articles/new-moms-fears.shtml#ixzz3S2P9eF36).

11. Dana's pediatrician later determined that Dana's ITP was most likely triggered by an antibiotic she'd been prescribed (by a different doctor) for an upper respiratory infection that was possibly viral, not bacterial. It was assumed the antibiotic didn't know what to fight in her body, so it attacked her own blood platelets. (It was also possible that it was caused by a rare reaction to the MMR vaccination, so she was declared immune to MMR and ordered not to repeat that series of shots.)

12. Sarah Young, *Jesus Calling* (Nashville, TN: Integrity Publishers, 2004), p. 7.

13. Young, *Jesus Calling*, p. 8.

14. Chambers, *My Utmost for His Highest*, January 2.

15. Chambers, *My Utmost for His Highest,* April 15.

16. Kevin Lehman, *Have a New Kid by Friday* (Grand Rapids: Revell, 2008), p. 49.

17. Cindi McMenamin, *God's Whispers to a Woman's Heart* (Eugene, OR: Harvest House, 2014), p. 160.

18. Thirteen years later, I wrote a book based on this poem and principle, *Letting God Meet Your Emotional Needs* (Eugene, OR: Harvest House, 2000).

19. The apostle Paul is one who comes to mind. His story of being a killer of Christ followers to becoming a major Christ-follower himself is found in Acts 9:1-31.

20. This story is found in Genesis 37 and 39–50.

21. Exodus 2:11-12, emphasis added.

22. Chambers, *My Utmost for His Highest,* July 28.

23. This story is found in Luke 15:11-32.

24. In Luke 15:10, Jesus said, "There is rejoicing in the presence of the angels of God over one sinner who repents."

25. Chambers, *My Utmost for His Highest,* January 2.

26. Chambers, *My Utmost for His Highest,* August 2.

27. A.W. Tozer, *We Travel an Appointed Way,* new ed. (Camp Hill, PA: Wingspread Publications, 2010), pp. 3-4.

Parting Words
of Encouragement

How has God helped you through this book? I would love to hear from you and encourage you, personally, and pray for you as well.

You can find me online at www.StrengthForTheSoul.com. Leave me a message that you were there and let me know how I can pray for you. I always respond to my readers.

You can also connect with me on Facebook at Strength For The Soul.

Or you can send me a letter at:
Cindi McMenamin
c/o Harvest House Publishers
990 Owen Loop North
Eugene, OR 97402

To contact me to speak for your group, email me at:
Cindi@StrengthForTheSoul.com

Other Harvest House Books
by Cindi McMenamin

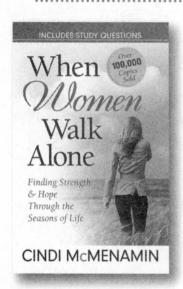

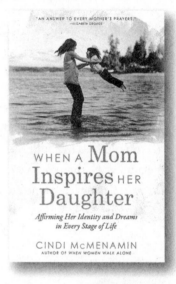

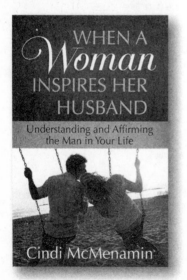

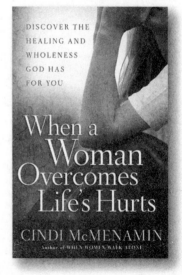